HISTORY, PHILOSOPHY AND SOCIOLOGY OF SCIENCE

Classics, Staples and Precursors

HISTORY, PHILOSOPHY AND SOCIOLOGY OF SCIENCE

Classics, Staples and Precursors

Selected By

YEHUDA ELKANA
ROBERT K. MERTON
ARNOLD THACKRAY
HARRIET ZUCKERMAN

THE DEFENSE OF GALILEO

Thomas Campanella

ARNO PRESS
A New York Times Company
New York — 1975

Reprint Edition 1975 by Arno Press Inc.

Reprinted from a copy in
  The Princeton University Library

HISTORY, PHILOSOPHY AND SOCIOLOGY OF SCIENCE:
Classics, Staples and Precursors
ISBN for complete set: 0-405-06575-2
See last pages of this volume for titles.

Manufactured in the United States of America

————◆————

Library of Congress Cataloging in Publication Data

Campanella, Tommaso, 1568-1639.
    The defense of Galileo.

    (History, philosophy and sociology of science)
    Translation of Apologia pro Galileo.
    Reprint of the 1937 ed. published by the Dept. of His-
tory of Smith College, Northampton, Mass., which was
issued as v. 22, no. 3-4 of Smith College studies in history.
    Bibliography: p.
    Includes index.
    1. Galilei, Galileo, 1564-1642. 2. Copernicus,
Nicolaus, 1473-1543. 3. Religion and science--Early
works to 1800. I. Title. II. Series. III. Series:
Smith College studies in history ; v. 22, no. 3-4.
QB36.G2C32 1975   215'.2   74-26254
ISBN 0-405-06582-5

VOL. XXII, Nos. 3-4   APRIL-JULY, 1937

Smith College Studies in History

WILLIAM DODGE GRAY
HAROLD UNDERWOOD FAULKNER
Editors

THE DEFENSE OF GALILEO
of Thomas Campanella

*For the First Time Translated and
Edited, with Introduction and Notes*

BY

GRANT McCOLLEY

NORTHAMPTON, MASS.
Published Quarterly by the Department of History of Smith College
Entered as second-class matter December 14, 1915, at the postoffice at Northampton,
Mass., under the act of August 24, 1912

CONTENTS

		PAGE
PREFACE	....	v
INTRODUCTION	....	vii
THE DEFENSE OF GALILEO	....	1
NOTES	....	76
INDEX	....	91

PREFACE

In translating the *Apologia pro Galileo* of Tommaso Campanella I have sought to make more widely known an important chapter in the seventeenth-century struggle for freedom of thought and investigation. There are few works of the era which depict so clearly the dominant issues in the controversy called forth by heliocentric astronomy, and none which challenge obscurantism with greater courage and virtuosity. It is fitting that this chapter should be republished on the eve of 1939, the tercentenary of the year when Campanella relinquished to other hands the torch of intellectual freedom.

I am indebted to the editors of the *Smith College Studies in History* for their courtesy in opening the series to a translation; to the University of Michigan Library for the copy of the Frankfort, 1622, edition of the *Apologia* from which the translation was made; and to Miss Mary Dunham, Librarian of Smith College, for her kindness in obtaining the further copy of the Frankfort edition employed in revision of the translation. Professors Douglas Bush, Lawrence Houtchens, Otto F. Kraushaar, Richard A. Rice, and William S. Taylor have contributed many helpful suggestions. Particularly heavy is my indebtedness to Professors Margaret B. Crook, Marjorie H. Nicolson, and Vincent M. Scramuzza for criticism and counsel. President William Allen Neilson has generously authorized the purchase of indispensable photostats. To these friends of the principles which Campanella championed in the *Defense of Galileo,* I express my gratitude.

Smith College   G. M.
June 1, 1938

INTRODUCTION

The *Defense of Galileo* was composed by Campanella in a Neapolitan dungeon during the year 1616, and was published at Frankfort in 1622 under the supervision of Tobia Adami.[1] It is a courageous and vibrant apology for freedom of investigation, for Copernican astronomy, and for the scientific method of the Florentine. Campanella challenges directly and in detail the major arguments which a powerful and determined ecclesiastical opposition had brought against the new philosophy, and demonstrates that these arguments are without adequate foundation. They were sired, he reiterates, by ignorance of Scripture and the works of the Fathers, by blind acceptance of pagan belief, and by the jealousy of clerics "who now they are called masters, are ashamed again to become disciples." The specific occasion which brought forth the *Defense* was the concerted attack upon both Galileo and heliocentric astronomy which developed rapidly following the *Sidereus Nuncius* or *Starry Messenger,* and culminated in proscription of the Copernican hypothesis. The initial step in the campaign of obscurantism was taken in May, 1611, when the Holy Office placed the name of Galileo on its list of suspects. Two years later the newly elected Professor of Mathematics at Pisa, Benedetto Castelli, was warned not to advocate the Copernican theory.[2] By 1615 professional enemies and over-zealous churchmen had driven Galileo to declare that every conceivable method of attack had been employed to discredit and ruin him.[3] In December of this year he was interrogated by the Inquisition at Rome, and ordered to renounce the Copernican hypothesis. Apparently doubtful of the efficacy of private admonitions, Cardinal Bellarmine prepared early in 1616 for ecclesiastical proscription

[1] The date of 1616 is supported by both internal and external evidence. In the *Defense* (p. 10), Campanella identifies the "present year" as "1616." On the 7 September, 1616, Jacopo Failla briefly described the apology in a letter to Galileo, and on 3 November, 1616, Campanella himself wrote Galileo regarding it. The two epistles are reproduced in *Le Opere di Galileo Galilei,* ed. Eugenio Albèri, Firenze, 1851, VIII, 391-2; 392-3.

[2] Castelli informed Galileo of this warning on 6 November, 1613 (*Le Opere,* VIII, 290-1).

[3] *Lettera a Cristina di Lorena,* as translated by Thomas Salusbury, *Mathematical Collections and Translations,* London, 1661, [I], 428.

of heliocentric astronomy. When word of this pending misfortune reached Campanella in his prison cell, he at once composed his spirited defense of Galileo and the new philosophy.[4] But the Holy Office had determined to act, and his plea, if heard, was not considered.[5] On 25 February, 1616, the Sacred Congregation of the Catholic Church officially condemned the *Revolutions* of Copernicus and Copernican astronomy.[6] On 5 March, the condemna-

[4] Evidence as to the month or months of composition is internal, and somewhat conflicting. In one passage (pp. 9-10) it is said that "Nolanus [Bruno], whose errors cannot be named, also supported the theory, as did other philosophers. (Nor were the heretics so much condemned for upholding the hypothesis; rather, Catholics were forbidden to read their books.) Outstanding among Copernican advocates is John Kepler . . . who defends the theory in his prefatory dissertation to the *Starry Messenger.*" . . . The parenthesized statement, which apparently refers to the proscription of Copernican astronomy by the Sacred Congregation, would seem to be an interpolation probably added by the Frankfort publisher. None of the several writers described by Campanella in this paragraph, Cusanus, Bruno, Kepler, Gilbert, and Maestlin, are mentioned in the decree. It is doubtful if the Catholic Campanella would have written, "rather, Catholics were forbidden to read their books." Certainly he would have described more accurately his Church's condemnation (*cf.* note 6, below). Equally important is the fact that continuity is improved by omission of the statement. Under such conditions, and in view of the evidence cited below, the comment apparently was not a part of the *Defense* as originally composed.

The persistent indications of hasty composition found in the apology: repetition of ideas, lack of continuity and organization within paragraphs, and contradictions seemingly caused by a failure to complete statements, suggest that the work was written rapidly. There existed no occasion for great haste after the proscriptive decree had been issued. Somewhat stronger evidence that the *Defense* was composed prior to the prohibition of Copernican astronomy is Campanella's declaration (p. 30), "I believe this kind of philosophy should not be prohibited. . . . Unless the new philosophy directly or indirectly opposes . . . the decrees of the Church, it clearly is not . . . inimical to Catholic doctrine." Equally if not more decisive is his concluding statement (p. 58), "Bellarmine himself declares that at this time heretics do not endanger Roman theology, and . . . it is unnecessary that the investigations of Galileo should be forbidden . . . a misfortune which is about to occur." To one writing the *Defense of Galileo,* there was but one event in the early months of 1616 which was connected with the head of the Holy Office and would be regarded as an occurrence about to take place. This was the official proscription of Copernican astronomy. It is of course possible that information as to the progress of events came slowly to Campanella, and that the decree had been issued shortly before the concluding lines of the *Defense* were written.

[5] Campanella was in part deeply troubled by the impending proscription because of his warm admiration for the achievement of Galileo. As Professor Nicolson has pointed out ("The Telescope and Imagination," *Modern Philology,* XXXII, 255-7), Campanella was among the first to realize the full significance of Galileo's discoveries, and he praised the Florentine as the one who had restored true philosophy (*Le Opere,* ed. Favaro, XI, 21-6).

[6] The decree of the Sacred Congregation is reprinted by Giovanni Battista Riccioli, *Almagestum Novum,* Bononiae, 1651, [II], 496. In keeping with the *Revolutions* of Copernicus, the *Commentary on Job* of Didacus

tion was formally announced, and printed copies prepared for distribution.

The *Defense of Galileo* was brought forth by an immediate and specific event, but the work is best understood against the background of the several movements with which it was intimately connected.[7] It will be of interest to survey briefly the life, contributions, and character of Campanella, together with the problems occasioned both by the nature and the growing prestige of heliocentric astronomy. The *Defense* itself played a significant part in the contemporary conflict over the authority in science of Scripture, and was linked with three important and closely allied movements: the emergence of modern empirical epistemology, the development of the idea of intellectual progress, and the controversy between "Ancients and Moderns." For perhaps a half century after its publication, Campanella's treatise was read by educated men throughout Europe, and to such intellectual and spiritual leaders as Bishops John Wilkins and John Amos Comenius, the *Apologia pro Galileo* gave a full measure of inspiration and encouragement.

I

Thomas Campanella was born 5 December, 1568, at Stilo in the province of Calabria, Italy. At the age of thirteen he had become an accomplished writer of verse and prose, and at fourteen his admiration for Albertus Magnus and Saint Thomas Aquinas led him to enter the Dominican Order. His philosophic allegiance soon passed however to the naturalistic thinker, Bernardino Telesio, in whose defense he wrote his first book, *Philosophia*

à Stunica was prohibited until so amended that the heliocentric hypothesis was presented purely as a theory. The last of the three books cited by the Sacred Congregation, the *Epistle* of Foscarini which the Frankfort printer refers to in the preface to the *Defense,* was prohibited and condemned *in toto.* By adding a blanket condemnation and prohibition of all works which supported the Copernican theory, the Sacred Congregation seriously handicapped Galileo in his increasingly successful advocacy of the hypothesis. To do this was apparently the principal immediate objective of the decree.

[7] Both the Introduction and the Notes which follow the text attempt to provide only the minimum of information essential to intelligent reading of the *Defense.* The interested student will find cited various books and articles which will provide somewhat detailed treatment of the ideas and movements discussed. The more extended quotations have been partially modernized in type usage, spelling, punctuation, and capitalization.

Sensibus Demonstrata, Naples, 1590. In the fashion of his day he attended various institutions, concluding his formal education at the University of Padua in 1595. As Pomponazzi and Telesio had done before him, Campanella vigorously attacked Aristotle as a menace to both religion and science, with the result that he was "detained" by the Holy Office. His release in 1597 brought only a brief period of freedom, and in less than two years he was charged with conspiracy to overthrow the Spanish government and establish a communistic commonwealth. While on trial before an ecclestiastical court, he was tortured and subjected to indignities by a civil tribunal, and at length sentenced to imprisonment for life. On 15 May, 1626, after twenty-seven years of confinement, he was paroled to the Holy Office and in 1629 granted complete liberty. A further Calabrian conspiracy threatened to involve him in 1634, but with the aid of Cardinal Barberini and the French ambassador he fled to the court of Louis XIII. Richelieu gave him a pension of 3000 livres, and King and Pope their favor. At the end of five years of peace he died in 1639 at the Dominican convent of St. Honoré in Paris.[8]

In his natural philosophy Campanella followed the animistic beliefs of Telesio, and postulated the existence of two opposing and attracting forces, one of expansion or warmth, the other of contraction or cold. The first has its seat in the Sun; the second in the earth. As was the case with other clerics of the period, Campanella's metaphysic embodied ideas definitely religious. All things which have existence, exist either as impulse or emanated

---

[8] The most complete account of the life and thought of Campanella is that of Alessandro D'Ancona, *Opere di Tommaso Campanella,* Torino, 1854, I, ix-cccxx. The most extended discussion of his philosophy provided by general histories will be found in 'Harald Höffding, *A History of Modern Philosophy,* London, 1924, I, 149-158 (Chapter XIV). Shorter accounts are given by Alfred Weber, *History of Philosophy,* tr. Thilly, New York, 1896, pp. 291-295; Frank Thilly, *A History of Philosophy,* New York, 1914, pp. 238-40; and B. A. G. Fuller, *A History of Philosophy,* New York, 1938, II, 43-4. An excellent study of Telesio is Neil C. Van Deusen, *Telesio: The First of the Moderns,* New York, 1932. Critical accounts of his life will be found in Francesco Fiorentino, *Bernardino Telesio, ossia studi storica su l'idea della natura nel Risorgimento italiano,* Firenze, 1872, I, 79-107, and Francesco Bartelli, *Note Biografiche,* Cosenza, 1906, pp. 7-73. In addition to brief comments in general histories of philosophy, and in encyclopaedias, the thought of Pomponazzi is discussed by G. Spieker, *Leben und Lehre des Petrus Pomponatius,* Munich, 1868, and F. Fiorentino, *Pietro Pomponazzi,* Firenze, 1868.

attraction; as force or power; or as knowledge or wisdom. Deity represents the greatest or infinite degree and form of power, and is active in all things. Being or existence is the capacity of an entity to make itself known or felt. Self-knowledge is immanent in our natures, but is continually obscured or perverted by external forces, with the result that we must learn of ourselves from our actions. The four proper objectives of mankind, he found, are the preservation of the individual self, perpetuation by means of children, renunciation of fame, and an eternal life with God, where man participates in infinite Being.

Volz is probably correct in his criticism that Campanella did not develop a philosophical system, but rather adapted and amplified the conclusions of others. We recall however that long imprisonment and repeated torture are scarcely conducive to highly organized intellectual achievement. Equally, if not more important was the transitional and disturbed state of thought during the first quarter of the seventeenth century. As Campanella confesses at the opening of the final chapter of the *Defense*, he had early constructed what we may term the foundation of a philosophic system, only to have basic postulates seriously weakened or made untenable by the discoveries of Galileo. That he should disregard his personal safety and courageously support the one who had shattered his beliefs is characteristic of the man.

Despite his understandable failure to erect a philosophic system of the first rank, Campanella was an original spirit who marched in the vanguard of modern thinkers. His portrayal of an ideal commonwealth, *The City of the Sun,* slightly anticipated *The New Atlantis* of Francis Bacon. His advocacy of direct observation and experimental study also preceded that of the Lord Chancellor.[9] From Augustine's doctrine that "as for me, the most certain of all things is that I exist," Campanella reached the point which, in the apparently later "cognito, ergo sum" of Descartes, became the foundation of Cartesian if not of modern philoso-

---

[9] Campanella's *City* or *Republic of the Sun* was published in 1623; *The New Atlantis,* incomplete when Bacon died in 1626, was published in 1629. The *Civitas Solis* or *La Citta' del sole* was translated into French and published in Paris in 1841. An English translation by Thomas W. Halliday will be found in Henry Morley's *Ideal Commonwealths* (3rd edition, London, 1887, pp. 217-263).

phy.[10] Since he regarded sensory experience as the primary basis of knowledge, the essentials of both his epistemology and method were those of the intellectual leaders of the seventeenth century.[11]

In his individualism, his eclecticism and catholicity of mind, as well as in his desire to take all knowledge as his province, Campanella was a true son of the Renaissance. Included among and often fused with his own beliefs are a multitude of ideas and conceptions drawn from a wide variety of sources: the Christian mystics, the Fathers and the scholastics, especially Albertus Magnus and Saint Thomas, the Jewish and Arabian schools, Pythagoras, Plato, Aristotle, Zeno, Empedocles, Copernicus, Telesio, and Galileo. We doubtless should question the encomium of the learned Cardinal Pallavicini, who described Campanella as "a man who had read and who remembered all things," but we may accept, I believe, the statement of a second contemporary, Vincent Baron, that he was a philosopher of "extraordinary gifts, skilled in mathematics, astrology, medicine, and other sciences."[12]

Although Campanella was a true son of the Renaissance and

[10] Campanella's *Metaphysics (Universalis philosophiae sive metaphysicarum rerum juxta propria dogmata partes III*, Paris, 1638) was not published until the year after Descartes' *Discours sur la méthode*, but as Höffding observes (*op. cit.*, I, 154), "there is no doubt that it was written for the most part while he [Campanella] was in prison."
[11] Various lists of Campanella's writings, some of which he provided, show that he composed eighty-eight works, many of which are preserved in MS. in the archives of the Dominican Order at Rome. Exclusive of those cited, the more important of his books are:
   (a) *Prodromus philosophiae instaurandae,* Frankfort, 1617.
   (b) *De sensu rerum et magia IV,* Frankfort, 1620.
   (c) *Realis philosophiae epilogisticae partes IV,* Frankfort, 1623.
   (d) *Astrologicorum libri VI,* Lyons, 1629.
   (e) *Atheismus triumphatus,* Rome, 1631.
   (f) *Medicinalium juxta propria principia libri VII,* Lyons, 1635.
   (g) *De praedestinatione, electione, reprobatione . . . . cento thomisticus,* Paris, 1636.
   (h) *Philosophiae rationalis partes V,* Paris, 1638.
[12] A discussion of the varied sources of Campanella's thought will be found in the works cited in note 8, above. An excellent brief account, with bibliography, may be had in the *Catholic Encyclopedia,* to which I am indebted for the quotations from Cardinal Pallavicini and Vincent Baron, as well as a number of the biographical details presented in the Notes. A standard history of the Renaissance in Italy is John Addington Symonds' *Renaissance in Italy,* 8 vols., New York, 1921-23. Two serviceable general histories of the period are Edward M. Hulme's *The Renaissance, the Protestant Revolution, and the Catholic Reformation in Continental Europe,* New York, 1923, and the *Cambridge Modern History,* I (Renaissance) and II (Reformation).

of the scientific movement which developed with it,[13] he was equally a faithful son of the Church. In the late sixteenth and early seventeenth centuries this meant nothing less than divided allegiance. The liberal Catholicism of earlier periods had surrendered to the intolerance and bigotry engendered and fed by reformation and counter-reformation. Moved by the political disorders of the time of Clement III, the sack of Rome by the troops of Charles V, the loss and danger of loss of extended territory, as well as the verbal attacks of enemies from without and the goading of friends from within, the Roman Church resorted to absolutism. With this came a more effective index of prohibited books, an ubiquitous Holy Office, and the doctrine of the supremacy of the Papacy. Supported largely by the powerful Dominican and Jesuit orders, there arose a new scholasticism whose objective was to establish the Church as the warden of truth and the one authority by which it could be determined. With the success of this movement the Holy Mother became "the guardian of thought, the guide of mind. She alone could judge what was truth and what error; what men ought to do or ought not to

[13] It has not been sufficiently recognized that the so-called modern scientific movement had definitely begun by the first part of the thirteenth century, and that for some time the influence of Aristotle generally favored the movement. His ideas were noticeably in advance of those which churchmen in general had advocated, or had dutifully repeated from such Fathers as Hippolytus, Eusebius, Theodoret, and Cosmas. Important in widening and deepening the growing scientific movement were the investigations of Albertus Magnus, the work of Roger Bacon and Raymond Lull, and the contributions of Jean Buridan, Bishop Oresme, Cardinal Cusanus, Leonardo da Vinci, Paracelsus, Andreas Vesalius, and Nicolaus Copernicus. Supporting and intensifying the spirit of scientific inquiry were the discoveries of Marco Polo, Columbus, Vasco da Gama, Magellan, and other voyagers. Discussion of the contributions and influence of these men will be found, among other places, in George Sarton, *Introduction to the History of Science,* Baltimore, 1931, II; Pierre Duhem, *Léonard de Vinci,* 3 vols., Paris, 1906-13, and *Le Système du Monde,* 5 vols., Paris, 1913-17; *Cambridge Medieval and Modern History;* W. Whewell, *History of the Inductive Sciences,* 3 vols., London, 1857 etc.; Kopp, *Ansichten über die Aufgabe der Chemie von Geber bis Stahl,* Braunschweig, 1875; Heller, *Geschichte der Physik,* Stuttgart, 1882; Höfer, *Histoire de la Chimie,* Paris, 1843; Hartmann, *Life of Paracelsus,* London, 1887; T. McCutcheon, *Paracelsus, University of Pennsylvania Lectures,* Philadelphia, 1916; Roth, *Andreas Vesalius,* Berlin, 1892; Portal, *Histoire de l'Anatomie et de la Chirurgie,* Paris, 1770; Meryon, *History of Medicine,* London, 1861; Haeser, *Lehrbuch der Geschichte der Medicin . . . ,* Jena, 1875 ff.; Sir William Osler, *The Evolution of Modern Medicine,* New Haven, 1921; Arturo Castiglioni, *Storia della Medicina,* Milan, 1936, and the histories of medicine of Cumston, London, 1926; Garrison, 4th ed., London, 1929; and Singer, Oxford, 1928.

know. . . . The new Scholastics converted their own church from the Catholicism which encouraged the Renaissance to the Romanism which suppressed it."[14] As a loyal son of this Church Campanella could say with all sincerity, "science is permitted to observe but the Church sits as the judge,"[15] and conclude his defense of Galileo with a formal statement of submission: "In the above discussion . . . I at all times submit myself to the correction and better judgment of our Holy Mother the Roman Church."

II

The great heresy of Copernican astronomy was that it invalidated a cosmology which had become an integral part of orthodox religious and philosophic thought. In this cosmology the earth stood immobile in the center of the universe. Above and moving about the earth were the Moon, Mercury, Venus, the Sun, Mars, Jupiter, Saturn, and the fixed stars, all of which were neatly placed in individual spheres or zones. Then followed the crystalline sphere and the primum mobile or prime mover. The latter turned the heavens and celestial globes in daily revolution about the central earth, and in some mysterious way provided the energy necessary for the remaining sidereal and planetary motions.[16] This limited and compact universe extended approximately one hundred and thirty million miles in its semidiameter, half of which was the depth of the sphere of the fixed stars. Adjoining and surrounding the mundane cosmos was the immobile Empyrean or Heaven of heavens, the abode of God and the angelic hierarchies.

In the center of the earth, and therefore at the greatest pos-

[14] *Cambridge Modern History*, II, 705.
[15] *Defense of Galileo*, Frankfort, 1622, p. 55.
[16] Some geocentric astronomers omitted the crystalline, and employed nine spheres; others utilized eleven or twelve. To each of the first eight spheres or zones, they ascribed two boundaries, with that nearer the earth known as the concavity of the sphere, and that farther removed as the convexity. During the sixteenth century an appreciable number of orthodox astronomers believed these spheres or zones contained one or more solid shells which imparted motion to the celestial bodies. I discuss the major variations of sixteenth and early seventeenth century Ptolemaic astronomy in some detail in "The Astronomy of *Paradise Lost*," *Studies in Philology*, XXXIV (1937), 222-8. A more extended treatment will be found, among other histories of astronomy, in J. L. E. Dreyer, *History of the Planetary Systems* . . . , Cambridge, 1906.

sible distance from God and Heaven was Hell and its ever-burn-
ing flames. Because our globe contained Hell, occupied the center
or most undignified place, and was composed of earth and water,
the lowest of the four elements, it was regarded, physically, as
the most inferior part of the creation. Its one claim to importance
was that it sustained man, and joined the stars in ministering to
him. The heavens, stars, and planets were made up of the noble
element of fire or the equally noble quintessence. Inhabiting the
stars and planets were such etherial beings as translated saints or
middle spirits. The Empyrean or Heaven of heavens encircled a
relatively small universe, so that God and the angels always were
near to man on earth. As the literal statement of Scripture demanded, the stars and Sun were mobile, the earth immobile, and
the "world" was enclosed by a firmament or shell. Because this
cosmology was inextricably combined with what passed for theology, any pronounced departure from it conflicted with the val-
ues established by religion as well as with accepted theories of
presumed science.

The heliocentric universe conceived by Copernicus was indeed a radical departure from orthodox cosmology. By exchang-
ing the places of earth and Sun, Copernicus brought earth and
the Hell within it into the pure heavens. By making the earth
one of the planets he prepared the way for the corollary that the
planets are earths. His belief that Sun and heaven are immobile,
and that all planets move in orbital revolution about the Sun,
dispensed with much of the celestial machinery so beloved by
the poet, theologian and astronomer of the sixteenth century. Because of the apparent absence of annual stellar parallax, Copernicus rightly described the stars of the eighth sphere as located
at an unmeasurable and almost infinite distance from the earth.[17]
He removed the bounding convexity which had enclosed the stars,

[17] By *annual stellar parallax* is meant a change in the relative positions
of the earth and two or more "fixed" stars occasioned by the annual orbital revolution of the earth about the Sun. With the earth moving about
the Sun, the only explanation for an (apparent) absolute lack of annual
stellar parallax, and the one advanced by Copernicus in the *Revolutions*,
I, x, is that the stars are so far from the earth that its annual orbit represents no more than a point in comparison with the distance to them. It
was not until 1838, almost two centuries after publication of the *Revolutions*, that annual stellar parallax was demonstrated by Bessel and others.

and declared the limits of the universe were not known and could not be known.[18] By extending almost to infinity the distance from earth to the fixed stars, and to an unknown and indefinite if not infinite distance the depth of this sphere, Copernicus completely disrupted the compact Ptolemaic cosmos, and divorced the abode of man from the Heaven of God and the angelic hierarchies.[19]

Perhaps more distressing to orthodox thought was the encroachment of the unbounded and unlimited universe of Copernicus upon the sacred realm assigned to Deity.[20] Heaven thus became a mixture of angels, translated saints, and giant suns. Our most compact illustration of this logic is provided by the usually objective Elizabethan scientist, Thomas Digges. In the explanatory diagram of *A Perfit Description of the Caelestiall Orbes according to the most aunciente doctrine of the Pythagoreans, latelye reuiued by Copernicvs* . . . , Digges says of the unbounded eighth sphere of Copernicus: "This orbe of starres fixed infinitely vp extendeth hit self in altitvde sphericallye, and therefore immovable [,] the pallace of foelicitye garnished with perpetvall shininge gloriovs lightes innvmerable, farr excellinge

---

[18] *De Revolutionibus Orbium Caelestium Libri VI,* I, viii, x (Thorn, 1873, pp. 21-2, 28-9). That Copernicus regarded the universe as unbounded is pointed out by the present writer in "The Seventeenth Century Doctrine of a Plurality of Worlds," *Annals of Science,* I (1936), 406 ff.; "Nicolas Copernicus and an Infinite Universe," *Popular Astronomy,* XLIV (1936), 525 ff.; and "The Eighth Sphere of *De Revolutionibus,*" *Annals of Science,* II (1937), 354 ff. Additional evidence will be found in "The Universe of *De Revolutionibus,*" forthcoming in *Isis.*

[19] As Professor Marjorie Nicolson has pointed out, "Milton and the Telescope," *English Literary History,* II (1935), 1-32, *passim,* Milton accepted and utilized in *Paradise Lost* (1667) the immeasurably expanded eighth sphere of post-Copernican and post-telescopic astronomy. In an apparently unguarded moment (III, 481 ff.), he nevertheless provides a striking illustration of the older conception of a compact cosmos wherein Heaven adjoined the mundane universe. His characters leave the earth, and:

> pass the planets seven, and pass the fixed,
> And that crystalline sphere whose balance weighs
> The trepidation talked [of], and that first moved;
> And now Saint Peter at Heaven's wicket seems
> To wait them with his keys . . .

[20] As Copernican astronomy increased in prestige and influence, the idea of a circular heaven gradually disappeared. In 1667 (Paradise Lost, II, 1047 ff.), Milton depicts Heaven, "undetermined square or round," as located "above" the cosmos.

ovr sonne both in qvantitye and qvalitye [—] the very covrt of coelestiall angelles . . . [and] the habitacle for the elect."[21]

Because of the many changes in conceptions both scientific and religious required by acceptance of the Copernican hypothesis, together with its author's inability to prove by stellar parallax the annual revolution of the earth, it is not surprising that for decades after 1543 heliocentric astronomy found few friends and fewer advocates. It so chanced however that in 1572 a new star appeared in the constellation of Cassiopeia. Here was visual proof that the heavens were alterable, and that orthodox astronomy was at the least incomplete.[22] Quite significantly, the new star suggested to Thomas Digges the Copernican hypothesis, and led him to make careful observations in the hope that he might connect its decline in brilliance with the orbital revolution of the earth.[23] Further evidence of the inadequacy of orthodox conceptions was provided by the comet of 1577. It had been thought that comets were not of celestial substance and so could not go above the moon, the sphere of which was considered the limit of the elementary world. But when Tycho Brahe (and Maestlin) traced the orbit of the comet, he found that it passed around the Sun outside the orbit of Venus. Not only had "elementary" substance entered the "pure" heavens of the Aristotelians, but it had passed unimpeded through the "solid" planetary spheres. When Tycho announced this discovery, he set forth a new astronomical hypothesis.[24] His theory differed markedly from that of Copernicus, and yet it employed the relative order he ascribed to the planets. Another advance had been made.

This more or less piecemeal acceptance of conceptions either

[21] Appendix to Leonard Digges, *A Prognostication euerlastingc* . . . London, 1576, f. 43.
[22] There were of course those who regarded the new star as a miracle not dissimilar to the star of Bethlehem. The appearance of a second new star in 1604, discussed below, largely discredited this supposition.
[23] *Alae seu Scalae Mathematicae,* London, 1573, sigs. L2ᵛ, 2A3ᵛ. The *Alae* of Digges is discussed in some detail by Francis R. Johnson and Sanford V. Larkey, "Thomas Digges," *Huntington Library Bulletin,* V (1934), 107 ff.
[24] *De Mundi Aetherei Recentioribus Phaenomenis* (1588, pp. 185 ff.), *Tychonis Brahe Dani Opera Omnia,* ed. J. L. E. Dreyer, Hauniae, 1922, IV, 155 ff. The standard biography, also by Dreyer, is *Tycho Brahe,* Edinburgh, 1890.

stressed or implicit in the hypothesis of Copernicus was further extended by a second book published in the year 1588, the *Fundamentum Astronomicum* of Nicolas Reymers. In this work Reymers added to the conceptions of Tycho mentioned above, the two theories that the earth rotates diurnally on its axis, and that the sphere of the fixed stars has no bounding convexity.[25] Each of these theories was emphasized a decade later in the *Magnet* of William Gilbert.[26] The appearance in 1604 of a second new star (on this occasion in the constellation of Serpentarius), again challenged the conventional belief in an immutable heaven.[27] As the star of 1572 had stimulated Thomas Digges to praise the Copernican hypothesis, so that of 1604 provided Kepler and Galileo with an opportunity to press its claims.[28] In 1609 and 1610 the telescope and *Starry Messenger* of Galileo demonstrated that the Moon is a physical body similar to our earth, and that Jupiter is encircled by four satellites.[29] Galileo also confirmed the assertion of Copernicus that a close and detailed observation of Venus would show the existence of phases identical to those of the Moon.[30] He discovered with other astronomers variable spots on the surface of the Sun, which proved it could not consist of the

[25] *Fundamentum Astronomicum*, Argentorati, 1588, fols. 37ʳ ff. I discuss Reymers' contributions in some detail in "Nicholas Reymers and the Fourth System of the World," *Popular Astronomy, XLVI* (1938), 25 ff.
[26] London, 1600, VI, 3 ff.
[27] A compact discussion of the profound reactions occasioned by the new stars of 1572 and 1604 will be found in "The Telescope and Imagination" of Professor Nicolson, *loc. cit.*, section I, and "The 'New Astronomy' and English Literary Imagination," *Studies in Philology*, XXXII (1935), section III (pp. 441 ff.).
[28] The standard biography of Galileo is J. J. Fahie, *Galileo*, London, 1903. A useful, but incomplete work on Kepler is the collection of essays prepared under the auspices of the History of Science Society under the title *Johann Kepler, 1571-1630* . . . , Baltimore, 1931.
[29] The *Starry Messenger* (*Sidereus Nuncius*) of Galileo was probably the most important book published during the first quarter of the seventeenth century. It was translated into English by E. S. Carlos in 1880, under the title *The Sidereal Messenger*.
[30] It is not infrequently stated that the phases observed in Venus proved the truth of the Copernican hypothesis. Unfortunately, they proved no more than the ancient geoheliocentric theory, revived with alterations by Tycho Brahe in 1588, according to which Venus and Mercury revolve about the Sun. This theory had received rather general acceptance prior to invention of the celestial telescope. The most complete discussion of its early history is that of Duhem, *Le Système du Monde*, ed. cit. A brief account will be found in "The Astronomy of *Paradise Lost*," *loc. cit.*, section IV.

pure celestial substance postulated by the Aristotelians, and that it rotates on its axis, as the earth was said to do.[31] The Milky Way was found composed of individual stars, far too numerous to be enclosed within the limited eighth sphere of Ptolemaic astronomy.

By the year 1615 it had been demonstrated that the planets do not consist of an immutable celestial essence but rather of physical material which at the least was comparable to that found in the earth. As the century reasoned, it therefore was possible for the earth to be a planet, and as Copernicus had said, for it to move in heaven. Since the Sun rotates on its axis, the earth might well do likewise. There also was a wide and growing acceptance of the Copernican planetary order and of the theory that Mercury and Venus revolve about the Sun, and a definite tendency to remove the bounding convexity of the Ptolemaic sphere of the fixed stars. The absence of stellar parallax, which Copernicus had attributed to the indefinite distance between earth and the fixed stars, remained the one valid scientific objection which could be brought against the heliocentric hypothesis. This objection had been seriously weakened by the magnitude of the new universe disclosed by the telescope. Moreover, Aristotelian-Ptolemaic astronomy was no longer respected by the majority of scientists and philosophers, and the adequacy of the Tychonic was seriously questioned.[32] In 1615 the Copernican theory had not been proved, but it stood as the most probable of the

[31] The greater portion of the discoveries announced by Galileo in the *Starry Messenger* and such supplementary discussions as the "Discourse on Floating Bodies" were confirmed and perhaps in part anticipated by Simon Mayer, Christopher Scheiner, and other contemporaries. They may be said to have been accepted by orthodox Catholic astronomers by the year 1620, when Josephus Blancanus (Giuseppe Biancani) published the first edition of the *Sphaera Mundi*.

[32] In the Tychonic hypothesis, the sphere of the fixed stars was regarded as closer to the earth (14,000 semidiameters) than in the Ptolemaic (approximately 20,000 semidiameters of the earth), and the earth was placed immobile in the center of the universe. Evidence provided by the telescope, particularly that of the nature of the Milky Way, made the first conclusion untenable. The second conclusion, which had for several decades prior to the telescope been severely criticized by advocates of the theory of the diurnal rotation of the central earth, was virtually invalidated by discovery of the axial rotation of the Sun and Jupiter. I discuss the history and importance of this hypothesis in "The Theory of the Diurnal Rotation of the Earth," *Isis*, XXVI (1937), 392-402, and "The Astronomy of *Paradise Lost*," *loc. cit.*, Section I.

several rival hypotheses. Vigorous opposition to the theory, and conversely, effective support of a geocentric and theologically orthodox cosmos could no longer be provided by astronomers. If cosmology were to continue an obedient handmaid of the Roman Church it was imperative that the Church should act. The result was proscription of heliocentric astronomy by decree of the Sacred Congregation.

III

Among the basic causes which led the Roman Church to support geocentric astronomy by proscriptive decree, perhaps the most vital was the conviction that Scripture, literally interpreted, provided the final word in cosmology.[33] If the judgment of Campanella may be trusted, this conviction was unquestionably the most fundamental, for he built the *Defense* around the question, "Is the kind of philosophy made famous by Galileo in harmony with or is it opposed to the Sacred Scriptures?" The conflict between Scriptural literalism and heliocentric astronomy was markedly intensified by the discoveries of Galileo, but it was not occasioned by them. It had existed and had been growing in vigor for many decades. In the *Narratio Prima* of 1539, Rheticus is clearly aware that Scriptural objections will be brought against heliocentric astronomy,[34] and in the *Revolutions* of 1543 Copernicus goes so far as to challenge these objections and to castigate those who may raise them.

If perchance there shall be idle talkers who, though . . . ignorant of all mathematical sciences, nevertheless . . . should dare to criticize and attack this hypothesis of mine, because of some passage of Scripture which they have distorted falsely for their

[33] The controversy between Scriptural literalism and heliocentric astronomy was but one chapter in an extended conflict between theology and science. The most comprehensive general treatment of this conflict is Andrew Dickson White, *A History of the Warfare of Science with Theology in Christendom,* 2 vols., 3rd ed., New York, 1928.

[34] "Universi distributio" (Thorn, 1873, p. 466). Rheticus spent two years (1539-41) with Copernicus at Frauenburg. The *Narratio Prima* was written during the first ten weeks of the extended visit. It is primarily a lengthy review of the *Revolutions,* but contains important additions probably based upon oral discussions with the author. The favorable reception given the *Narratio Prima* was the chief influence which caused Copernicus to permit the *Revolutions* to be published. There was however an unfortunate sequel, for his friendship with Copernicus and advocacy of heliocentric astronomy cost Rheticus his professorship at the University of Wittenberg.

purposes, I care not at all—I will even despise their judgment
as foolish. It is not unknown that Lactantius, otherwise an able
writer . . . speaks most foolishly regarding the shape of the
earth when he ridicules those who said it has the form of a
sphere.[35]

Because Copernicus presented this challenge in his dedicatory
preface to Pope Paul III, he obviously feared the opposition of
Roman Catholics. It was however the Protestants who first became vocal. Indeed, the dynamic leader of the German reformation, Martin Luther, had vigorously castigated Copernicus at
least four years prior to publication of the *Revolutions.* "A
new astrologer is risen," he declared, "who presumeth to prove
that the earth moveth and goeth about, not the Firmament, the
Sun, Moon, nor the Stars. . . . This fool will turn the whole
art of Astronomie upside down, but the Scripture sheweth and
teacheth him another lesson, where Joshua commanded the Sun
to stand still and not the earth.[36] Although less denunciatory than
Luther, Calvin was equally certain that Scripture represented the
final word in astronomy, and in his *Commentary on Genesis* cited
the first verse of the ninety-third Psalm and inquired, "Who will
venture to place the authority of Copernicus above that of the Holy
Spirit?"[37] More extended, but similar in conclusion, is the comment of Melanchthon, who devoted an entire section of the *Initia
Doctrinae Physicae* to attacks upon heliocentric astronomy. It was
his conviction that the Copernican theory affected adversely the
status of man, and perhaps more importantly, contradicted various
passages in Psalms and Ecclesiastes.[38] He could find nothing good
or desirable in the hypothesis:

The eyes are witnesses that heaven revolves in twenty-four
hours. Yet certain men, either because they love novelty or desire to make a display of ingenuity, have asserted that the earth
moves, and maintain that neither the Sun nor the eighth sphere

[35] Preface (ed. cit., p. 7). The standard biography of Copernicus is
Leopold Prowe, *Nicolaus Coppernicus,* 2 vols., Berlin, 1883-4.
[36] *Colloquia Mensalia, or His Divine Discourses at His Table,* London,
1659, p. 503 (*Werke,* Weimar, 1912, *Tischreden,* I, no. 855; IV, no. 4638).
[37] I present a more detailed analysis of the late sixteenth and seventeenth century conflict between Scriptural literalism and the new astronomy
in "The Ross-Wilkins Controversy," *Annals of Science,* III (1938),
153-189.
[38] Liber I, "Quis est Motus Mundi " (Vitebergae, 1657, fols. 40ʳ ff.).

revolves. . . . It is a want of decency and honesty to declare publicly such notions, and the example is pernicious. It is the proper part of a good mind to accept truth as it is revealed by God, and to acquiesce in it.

During the final quarter of the sixteenth century the practice of rejecting and attacking the new astronomy because of its incompatibility with Scripture became increasingly common, and made its way into the works of professional Catholic astronomers. It was followed in the most authoritative and widely used commentary on Sacro Bosco, one extant in many editions between 1581 and 1611, the *In Sphaeram Ioannis de Sacro Bosco Commentarius* of Christopher Clavius. The position taken by this influential Jesuit is representative of that commonly found among orthodox communicants of the Roman Church:

Si vero dicatur terra moveri super alium axem. . . . Favent huic quoque sententia sacrae literae quae plurimis in locis terram esse immobilem affirmant. Solemque ac caetera astra moveri testantur; Legimus enim in Psalmo 103: "Qui fundasti terram super stabilitatem suam, non inclinabitur in seculum seculi." Item in Ecclesiaste cap. I: "Terra in aeternum stat, oritur Sol, & occidit, & ad locum suum revertitur, ibique renascens gyrat per meridiem, & flectitur ad aquilonem." Quid clarius dici poterat? Clarissimum quoque testimonium, quod Sol moveatur, perhibit nobis Psalmus 18, in quo ita legitur: "In sole posuit tabernaculum suum, & ipse tanquam sponsus procedens de thalamo suo, exultavit ut Gigas ad currendam viam, a summo caelo egressio eius; Et occursus eius usque ad summum eius, nec est qui se abscondat a calore eius." Rursus inter miracula refertur, quod Deus aliquando Solem aut retroduxit, aut prorsus, ut consisteret, effecit.[39]

Nor were professional Catholic astronomers and mathematicians alone in rejecting the heliocentric theory because of adherence to the literal word of Scripture. In complete agreement with Clavius was the important Protestant astronomer, Tycho Brahe. Tycho not only found the Copernican hypothesis unacceptable because of its conflict with Holy Writ, but went so far as to assert that since Moses called the Moon the lesser light, he must have known astronomy.[40] A decade after Tycho, the Englishman Thomas Hill declared that "Both holy Scriptures

---

[39] *Commentarius*, Romae, 1585, pp. 196-7; Moguntiae, 1611, *Opera*, III, 106.

[40] *Tychonis Brahe Dani Epistolae Astronomicae*, p. 148; *Opera*, ed. J. L. E. Dreyer, VI, 177 ff.

confirme and Phisicke reasons proove. . . . Earth abideth fixed and unmoveable in the myddle of the world."[41] Hill then cited in the somewhat unusual order of Clavius the three passages from Psalms, Ecclesiastes, and Psalms quoted by the Jesuit astronomer.

English attacks upon the Copernican hypothesis were not confined to the strictures of astronomers and mathematicians. In 1612 the Prebendary of Salisbury, Nicholas Fuller, presented in his *Miscellaneorum Theologicorum Libri III* a detailed list of Scriptural texts which assert the mobility of the Sun and heavens and the immobility of the earth.[42] Much less widely read, but equally indicative of the vogue of literalism was the *Briefe Discovery* of Fuller's friend and colleague, William Barlow, Archdeacon of Salisbury.[43] The immediate objection of Barlow's attack is his contemporary Marke Ridley, but his devotion to the word of Scripture is none the less obvious:

[Ridley] must be ruled by reason, and affoord all those his patience that do beleeve the holy Scriptures, which flatly denie the Earths motion, and affirme the motion of the Sunne, Moone & Stars, in the whole current thereof, as *Psal. 19.6; 104.5; Iosua 10.12.13.14; Esay* [Isaiah] *38.8. &c.* . . . [He] will not be offended with those who do pitifully laugh at his Magneticall Astronomy, with those topsiturvy motions. . . . But although such [reasons] as these are, may goe current in a mechanicall Trades-man shop, yet they are very insufficient to bee allowed for good, by men of learning and Christians by profession. . . . And that which we call Nature, it being nothing else but God's ordinance. . . . God hath ordained the motion of the Sunne, Moone, and Stars . . . and the unmooveablenesse of the earth.[44]

[41] *The Schoole of Skil*, London, 1599, p. 49.
[42] This first edition of three books was published in Heidelberg, 1612. Fuller's attack upon heliocentric astronomy occurs in Book I, Chapter XV (Strassburg, 1650, pp. 94 ff.).
[43] Other illustrations of English literalism are the remarks of Thomas Overbury (*Works,* ed. Rimbault, London, 1856, p. 271), "Astronomy was first taught by God . . . and therefore the first must needs have been the most excellentest," and of Samuel Purchas (*His Pilgrimage,* London, 1613, pp. 8 ff.). Purchas concludes his evaluation of Copernican and other astronomers with the statement, "As for all such strange and phantasticall or phreneticall opinions of Heretikes, or Philosophers, which have otherwise related of this mysterie of the Creation, then Moses, they need not confuting."
[44] *A Briefe Discovery of the Idle Animadversions of Marke Ridley* (British Museum photostat in the library of Smith College), London, 1618, pp. 6-9.

Among continental advocates of the authority of Holy Writ in astronomy, Helisaeus Roeslin in 1597 rejected the Copernican hypothesis on the grounds that it was "contrary to experience, to physics, and to Sacred Scripture."[45] Two years after publication of the *Starry Messenger,* Julius Caesar la Galla in part challenged the theory because it controverted the Bible.[46] A third writer, the celebrated theologian Pineda, paused to censure heliocentric astronomy in two commentaries, one on Job, the other on Ecclesiastes. In the first, published 1608, Pineda replied to the argument of Didacus à Stunica that Job 9.6 supported the Copernican theory, and asserted that on the contrary the passage proved the earth's immobility.[47] In the commentary on Ecclesiastes, published in 1619 but completed several years earlier, he not only answered Didacus and challenged both the Copernican hypothesis and the theory of the diurnal rotation of the central earth, but multiplied Scriptural citations against the two conceptions. He began with Ecclesiastes 1.4, which he was expounding, moved to Job 9.6, discussed by him in the previous commentary, and next to Job 26.7 and 38.4. Among others, he then presented four passages from Psalms, and verses from 2 Kings, Isaiah, and Ecclesiastes.[48]

It was inevitable that advocates of the Copernican and related theories should challenge those who proclaimed Scripture, literally construed, the final authority in astronomy. As a result, conflict over the mobility of the earth became to an important degree conflict over the interpretation of Scripture. Catholic and Protestant, cleric and layman, declared abroad their variant glosses of Biblical passages, and Holy Writ was tossed and buffeted on the winds of controversy. Such a situation threatened both the prestige of Scripture and the dogma that the Roman Church was the sole judge of its meaning.

[45] *De Opere Dei Creationis, seu de Mundo Hypotheses* . . . no place or date (first edition, Frankfort, 1597), Appendix, p. 76.
[46] *De Phoenomenis in Orbe Lunae,* Venice, 1612, Chapter VII.
[47] *Commentariorum in Job Libri Tredecim,* 1608; Venice, 1739, I, 252-3.
[48] *In Ecclesiasten Commentariorum Liber Unus,* 1619; Antwerp, 1920, pp. 108 ff. The book was approved by "Facultas R. P. Provincales" in December, 1617. Since no mention is made of the proscriptive decree of the Sacred Congregation of 5 March, 1616, it may be assumed that at least the portion of the commentary which dealt with Ecclesiastes 1.4 had been completed prior to March, 1616.

The serious conflict which developed over interpretation of the Bible was foreshadowed in 1590, when Christopher Rothmann differed sharply with his friend Tycho Brahe regarding the authority of Scripture in astronomy.[49] Their discussion also indicated that the controversy would bring in review passages in Scripture unrelated to Copernicanism, for in it Rothmann pointedly asked Tycho if he believed in the windows of heaven, for the reason that these windows are mentioned in the account of the Flood.[50] More significant, in the sense that it came before more readers, was Edward Wright's prefatory epistle to Gilbert's *De Magnete*. His invocation of the doctrine of accommodation was entirely conventional, but his use of it in defense of the motion of the earth was quite the contrary. "It was not," he declared, "the purpose of Moses or the Prophets to set forth any mathematical or physical subtleties, but rather to accommodate themselves to the understanding of the vulgar and to ordinary methods of speech, much as nurses are accustomed to accommodate themselves to their infants."[51] In the slightly later *De Mundo nostro Sublunari Philosophia Nova,* Gilbert himself directly censured literalism, and said in part: "Although it is urged that the earth is not moved because of the testimony of Psalm 74, 'I have established the borders [*columnas*] of the earth,' the Sacred Book accommodates its phrases to human capacity."[52] As he continued, Gilbert likewise rejected the authority of two of the passages frequently emphasized by the literally orthodox: "He hath established the earth; it shall not be moved," and, "The earth abideth forever."

In the years 1609 and 1615 there followed the important challenges to literalism enunciated by Kepler, Foscarini, and Galileo. To his denial of the assumption that moot passages in Scripture

---

[49] In his *Commentary upon Job,* Chapter IX, verse vi (Toledo, 1584, pp. 205 ff.), Didacus à Stunica sought to reconcile Scripture with Copernican astronomy, and in 1597 Nicolas Reymers made in his *De Astronomicis Hypothesibus . . .* (Prague, 1597, sigs. E^r ff.) a similar attempt with reference to the diurnal rotation of the earth. However, Reymers declared that the Copernican hypothesis was contrary to Scripture.

[50] *Epistolae Astronomicae,* p. 129; *Opera,* ed. cit., VI, 158-9.

[51] *De Magnete,* London, 1600, Preface.

[52] Amstelodami, 1651, p. 163. The work was necessarily written before 1603, the year of Gilbert's death.

were intended by the Holy Ghost to be literally true, Kepler added vigorous comment upon the fallibility of important Saints:[53]

There are very many [men] who are so devoted to Holiness, that dissent from the Judgment of *Copernicus,* fearing to give the Lye to the Holy Ghost speaking in the Scriptures, if they should say, that the Earth moveth, and the Sun stands still. But . . . many things daily occur, of which we speak according to the Sense of Sight, when as we certainly know that the things themselves are otherwise. . . . And thus much concerning the Authority of Sacred Scripture. Now as touching the opirions of the Saints about these Natural Points. I answer in one word, That in Theology the weight of Authority, but in Philosophy the weight of Reason is to be considered. Therefore Sacred was *Lactantius,* who denied the Earth's rotundity; Sacred was *Augustine,* who granted the Earth to be round, but denied the *Antipodes;* Sacred is the Liturgy of our Moderns, who admit the smallnesse of the Earth, but deny its Motion: But to me more sacred than all these is Truth.[54]

With the appearance of the *Epistle* of Foscarini, the conflict over the authority of Scripture, literally interpreted, entered its final stage. Earlier opponents had confined themselves to short refutations included in scientific or theological works. The *Epistle* however was a relatively extended treatise devoted primarily to an organized and carefully developed attack upon literalism. It discusses in six classes "all authorities of Divine Writ which seem to oppose" the heliocentric hypothesis. Of these several classes the last is "rather of Fathers and Divines, than of the Sacred Scriptures." The two initial groups consist of the direct statements which (1) "affirm the earth to stand still" and (2) "attest the sun to move." The remaining classes are those which describe Hell as located in the center of the world and in the center of the earth. According to the first opinion, said Foscarini, it follows from the Copernican theory that Hell is in the sun. If we suppose "Hell is in the Center of the Earth, [and] if the Earth should move about the Sun, it would necessarily ensue that Hell,

---

[53] Kepler's indirect attack upon the authority in science of important Saints doubtless was suggested by Copernicus's censure of Lactantius, quoted above.

[54] *Astronomia nova* . . . Prague, 1609, as translated by Thomas Salusbury, *op. cit.,* p. 467.

together with the Earth, is in Heaven."[54a] His conclusion was that in describing physical phenomena, Holy Scripture followed the "commune and vulgar" way of speaking. The impact upon orthodoxy of Foscarini's urbane but logically devastating treatise is best illustrated by the decree of the Sacred Congregation that the *Revolutions* of Copernicus and the *Commentary upon Job* of Didacus were suspended until corrected, but that "librum vero P. Pauli Antonii Foscarini Carmelitae omnino prohibendum, atque damnandum."[55]

Similar in purpose and emphasis to the *Epistle* of Foscarini was the extended "letter" which Galileo addressed to the Grand Duchess Cristina di Lorena.[56] Its forthright declarations could not but irritate ecclesiastical authority, and Galileo's impeachment of both the integrity and intelligence of those who differed with him may have made doubly objectionable his error as a Roman Catholic layman in presenting his personal interpretation of Holy Writ:

They persisting therefore in their first Resolution of ruining me and whatsoever is mine . . . for these respects, I say, they have resolved to try whether they could make a Shield . . . of a feigned Religion and of the Authority of the Sacred Scriptures, applyed by them with little judgment. . . . And first, they have indeavoured . . . to divulge an opinion . . . that those Propositions [that earth moves etc.] are contrary to the Holy Letters, and consequently Damnable and Heretical . . . [But the statements that earth stands and the Sun is moved] were in that manner pronounced by the Sacred Scriptures that they might be accommodated to the Capacity of the Vulgar, who are very rude and unlearned. . . . And this is a doctrine so true and common amongst Divines, that it would be superfluous to produce any attestation thereof. . . . This therefore being granted, methinks that in the Discussion of Natural Problems, we ought not to begin at the authority of places of Scripture; but at Sensible Experiments and Necessary Demonstrations: For, from the Divine Word, the Sacred Scripture and Nature did both alike proceed.

[54a] Paolo Antonio Foscarini, *Epistle To Sebastianus Fantonus,* as reprinted and translated by Salusbury, *op. cit.,* pp. 474 ff. The translation is 37 folio pages in length.
[55] As reprinted by Riccioli, *op. cit.,* II, 496.
[56] The *Epistle of Galileo,* which occupies 40 folio pages in Salusbury's translation, was first published in 1636. I am unaware of the extent to which it was circulated in MS. prior to the decree promulgated by the Sacred Congregation on 5 March, 1616 [n.s.].

. . . Nor doth God less admirably discover himself unto us in Nature's Actions than in the Scriptures' Sacred Dictions. Which peradventure *Tertullian* intended to express in those words . . . God is known first by Nature, and then again more particularly known by Doctrine. . . . The prohibiting of the whole Science, what other would it be but an open contempt of an hundred Texts of the Holy Scriptures, which teach us that the Glory and the Greatnesse of Almighty God is admirably discerned in all his Works, and divinely read in the *Open Book* [my italics] of Heaven.[57]

By the close of the year 1615, the authority in astronomy of the literal word of Scripture had been severely challenged, and in some measure invalidated. There had developed an international conflict so bitter that it threatened the prestige of Scripture and the Fathers, and encroached upon the dogma that the Roman Church was the sole interpreter of Holy Writ. The accumulating scientific support of heliocentric astronomy, and the virtual destruction by Galileo of the foundations of opposing systems had left the Copernican hypothesis without an effective rival. If the Church wished to maintain its position as the one guardian of truth, and to end the conflict which raged over the meaning of Biblical passages, it could not remain inactive. Particularly if it desired to preserve the geocentric and compact universe made sacred by Scripture, by the Fathers, and by Roman theology, the Church must intervene.

We can only praise Campanella for his gallant attempt to halt the impending condemnation of heliocentric astronomy. He could not however hope for its success. The *Defense* is the most brilliant and daring of contemporary apologies, but it followed the *Epistles* of Foscarini and Galileo in placing the demonstrations of science above the words of Scripture and the conclusions of the Fathers. It described the opposition as envious and bigoted, as ignorant of both Scripture and the Fathers, and as men who worshipped the pagan Aristotle rather than the living Christ. The brilliance and daring of the *Defense* could only precipitate, not delay or prevent, the proscriptive action of the Church.

[57] *Epistle to Her Serene Highnesse Christina Lotheringa* . . . , as translated by Salusbury, *op. cit.*, pp. 428 ff. I am indebted to the John Crerar Library, Chicago, for its courtesy in permitting use of the Salusbury through interlibrary loan.

IV

Closely associated with the attack upon the authority of Scripture in science were three additional movements, the rise of an empirical theory of knowledge, the effective development of the idea of intellectual progress, and the successful rebellion of heterogeneous groups known as "Moderns" against others equally heterogeneous termed the "Ancients." Neither empirical epistemology, the idea of intellectual progress, nor rejection of ancient authority originated in the late sixteenth and early seventeenth centuries, but it was during this period that these movements began to achieve noticeable importance. The rôle which Campanella played in their development is less striking than his place in the revolt against Scriptural literalism, but is not without significance.

A

It had been an axiom of the Scholastics that there were no ideas in the human mind which had not entered through sensation. This axiom provided an entirely adequate foundation for an empirical epistemology, but by the scholastics it was neglected far more than it was applied. Their thought was in addition so dominated by Revelation and Roman theology, to say nothing of the Christianized Greeks, that effective application of the principle was impossible. The dynamic force which occasioned the development of a relatively empirical epistemology during the sixteenth and seventeenth centuries was not therefore the axiom or concept upon which this epistemology rests. It consisted rather in the growing scientific movement which gave increasing application to the principle, and occasioned its partial emancipation from Scripture, theology, and what loosely may be termed Aristotelian philosophy.[58]

[58] The conflict over Copernican astronomy had at first the curious result of increasing the prestige of the "testimony of sense" among opponents of the theory and of lessening its validity among advocates. As late as 1661, Joseph Glanvill argued in the *Scepsis Scientifica* (p. 77) that the apparent diurnal revolution of heaven did not disprove the heliocentric hypothesis because "the testimony of sense is weak and frivolous." Subsequent to invention of the telescope, the certainty of scientifically employed sensory observation was more and more urged by advocates of the theory.

In the modern empirical theory of knowledge developed by Locke, the "great source of most of the ideas we have" is sensation, or the information brought to the mind by the senses.[59] Sensation or perception is in fact the primary basis of all ideas, for, declared Locke, "To ask at what time a man has first any ideas, is to ask when he begins to perceive; having ideas and perception being the same thing." Exclusive of the reflection by which "the mind furnishes the understanding with ideas of its own operations," this epistemology is in essence a description of the emerging scientific method which made direct sensory observation the foundation of truth. As such, it is the natural culmination of a movement which more and more turned from sacred and profane books about nature to what Paracelsus, Galileo, and Campanella repeatedly called the book of nature. Standing alone, the emphasis upon the value and necessity of evidence obtained through the senses would have produced observations no more dependable than those recorded either in Scripture or the Fathers. The evidence was however gathered more carefully, and after invention and development of microscope and telescope was much more comprehensive and accurate. The evaluation of phenomena disclosed by the senses became more critical or scientific. Equally important was the awareness of such men as Rheticus, Kepler, Bacon, and Galileo that "he who investigates must have a free mind."[60]

Perhaps the first philosopher of the sixteenth century to stress the claims of empiricism was Leonardo da Vinci. He rejected all theorizing unconfirmed by experience, and regarded perception as the origin of all science. To him the data provided by the senses must be criticized by and combined with exact thought.[61] A second important figure was Copernicus. In discarding the complicated Ptolemaic system and establishing his superior and some-

[59] *Essay Concerning Human Understanding,* II, i, 3. The two subsequent quotations will be found II, i, 9 and 5.
[60] Georg Joachim Rheticus, *Narratio Prima,* ed. cit., p. 490. The comparable statements by Kepler and Galileo (*Le Opere,* ed. Albèri, VII, 55) are quoted by Höffding, *op. cit.,* I, 104. This belief is, I believe, implicit in Bacon's discussion of the "Idols which beset men's minds" (*Magna Instauratio, Aphorisms* [I], 39 ff.).
[61] *Cf.* Fuller, *op. cit.,* II, 12 ff.; Höffding, *op. cit.,* I, 164 ff.; Duhem, *Léonard . . . ,* ed. cit.

what less involved hypothesis, he apparently was deeply influenced by the principle that nature does nothing in the more difficult way. It is noteworthy however that in 1514 he declined an invitation to discuss the reform of the Calendar because he did not believe celestial phenomena had yet been sufficiently investigated. He mentions in the *Revolutions* that he frequently determined the obliquity of the ecliptic, and during the years 1497-1529 made twenty-seven observations to compute better the orbits of the planets.[62]

Subsequent to Copernicus, the validity and the necessity of employing sensory perception were supported by Paracelsus, Ramus, and Telesio.[63] Ramus urged an astronomy which was constructed, not from hypotheses, but from observations. Telesio declared he would found his philosophy on sensory experience alone, and established as his motto, *non ratione, sed sensu*. Somewhat later Bacon proclaimed eloquently the value of experiment and induction.[64] Prior to and during the period of Verulam's effective literary espousal of the principle of induction, Cardan, Tycho Brahe, Reymers, Gilbert, Kepler, Galileo and others were giving it increasing application. One of the greatest triumphs of astronomy, the discovery of the eliptical orbit of Mars, resulted from the happy combination of the accurate observations made by Tycho and their skillful use and analysis by Kepler. Together with the latter, Galileo emphasized the necessity of establishing quantitative relationships, and made phenomena the judge of all hypotheses.[65] Subsequent to publication of the *Starry Messenger* of Galileo and the rapid increase of telescopes in Europe, the practice of making observation both the foundation and the judge of theory became widespread among natural philosophers.

To Campanella, who had followed Telesio in seeking a philosophy based on perception, the *Starry Messenger* and telescope of

[62] *Cf.* Dreyer, *History,* ed. cit., pp. 305 ff.
[63] *Cf.* McCutcheon, *op. cit.,* pp. 461 ff.; Dreyer, *History,* pp. 358 ff.; Höffding, *op. cit.,* I, 93 ff.
[64] In the *Magna Instauratio, Aphorisms* [I], 1, Bacon states that man "can do and understand so much and so much only as he has observed in fact or in thought of the course of nature; beyond this he neither knows anything nor can do anything."
[65] An excellent brief discussion of Galileo's conception of scientific methodology will be found in Höffding, *op. cit.,* I, 176 ff.

Galileo brought a promise that his hope could be fulfilled.[66] He found sensory observation the indisputable foundation of "secular" truth, and declared in effect it would lead to absolute truth. Not only did he regard the testimony of sense as presented by Galileo far superior to the "opinion" of Aristotle, but considered it sufficiently authoritative to be trusted in interpreting Scripture:[67]

P. 30. Error cannot be found in Galileo. He does not deal with opinion, but builds his hypothesis upon careful observations from the book of the world.

P. 33. Galileo . . . prudently describes natural phenomena according to the testimony of observation . . . not . . . as conjecture may dictate, or, to follow Aristotle, as he may create from his own mind.

P. 35. Galileo demonstrates the truth of his doctrine by sensory observation.

P. 50. We therefore should praise Galileo, who after many centuries has by sensory experiments rescued Scripture from ridicule and distortion.

P. 50. We know that [by the discoveries of Galileo] Scripture is explained without violence and torture and false imaginations.

P. 52. Galileo . . . demonstrates not by imagination but by sensory observation.

In the *Defense,* Campanella not infrequently attempts to follow Galileo's scientifico-empirical method of observation and critical evaluation of data, but from a scientific point of view the results must be regarded as unfortunate. One effort to build upon the discoveries of Galileo did lead however to a curious consequence. On the basis of the Florentine's observations, particularly regarding the earth-like nature of the Moon, Campanella conjectured that Moon and stars are inhabited. Assisted by passages in Ephesians and Colossians, he then speculated concerning the nature of astral inhabitants.[68] Some two decades later John Wilkins summarized these speculations in his *Discovery of a World in the Moone,* and in evaluating them set forth the primary prin-

---

[66] The enthusiastic reception which Campanella gave to the discoveries of Galileo is discussed by Professor Nicolson, "The Telescope and Imagination," *loc. cit.* section IV.

[67] The pagination employed is that of the original Frankfort edition of 1622, as indicated by brackets in the present translation.

[68] *Defense,* pp. 51-2.

ciple of the empirical epistemology which Locke presents in his *Essay Concerning Human Understanding*:

> Wherefore Campanella's second conjecture may be more probable, that the inhabitants of that world [the Moon] are not men as we are, but some other kind of creatures which bear some proportion and likeness to our natures; or it may be they are of quite a different nature from anything here below, such as no imagination can describe, *our understandings being capable only of such things as have entered by our senses, or else such mixed natures as may be composed from them* [my italics].[69]

It is of further interest that Locke's essay was brought forth by speculations related to the type of conjecture which had led Wilkins to anticipate the basic principle of his theory of knowledge. Höffding has noted (II, 380) that James Tyrell, a friend of Locke, described the *Essay* as having been provoked by discussions concerning "the principles of morality and revealed religion." Locke himself does not identify the motivating speculations, but it would seem obvious from his Introduction, Section 7 that, as his friend declared, they involved religion:

> Occasion of this Essay. This was that which gave the first rise to this Essay concerning the Understanding. For I thought that the first step towards satisfying several inquiries the mind of man was very apt to run into, was, to take a survey of our own understandings, examine our own powers, and see to what things they were adapted. Till that was done, I suspected we began at the wrong end . . . whilst we let loose our thoughts into the vast ocean of being; as if all that boundless extent were the natural and undoubted possession of our understandings. . . . Thus men, extending their inquiries beyond their capacities, and letting their thoughts wander into those depths where they can find no sure footing, it is no wonder that they raise questions and multiply disputes, which . . . are proper only to continue and increase their doubts, and to confirm them at last in perfect scepticism.[70]

[69] *Discovery* . . . (first edition, 1638), London, 1640, pp. 189-90.
[70] For the interpretation that what may be termed materialistic utilitarianism was the force which moved Locke to write the *Essay*, see Robert K. Merton, "Science, Technology, and Society in Seventeenth Century England," *Osiris*, IV, 2 (1938), 589. Professor Merton says in part: "A deep-rooted utilitarianism is basic in Hobbes' philosophy. 'The end of knowledge is power; and . . . the scope of all speculation is the performance of some action, or thing to be done.' . . . Locke is, if possible, even more emphatic in this respect. Man should concern himself with the pursuit of only such knowledge as 'may be of use to us' . . . [footnote] *Essay*

The acceptance of an empirical epistemology which gave sensory observation precedence over the word of Scripture suggests to a modern age a general rejection of the authority of Holy Writ. Such was not the case during the period reviewed. Scripture remained to Campanella the basic source for theological truth.[71] As much may be said of Galileo, of Wilkins in 1640, of Locke in 1690, of Boyle, and of other advocates of an empirical theory of knowledge.[72] As Campanella had asserted that the demonstrations of science protected Scripture against distortion, so Locke declared adherence to scientific method in thought would prevent scepticism. It also was the hope of Campanella, as it was later the partially realized hope of Newton and Boyle, that religion and science might live together as mutually helpful peers, each contributing to and enlightening the other.[73]

. . . Introduction, section 5." Locke's expression, "may be of use to us," occurs in the following setting:

"[Section] 4. Useful to Know the Extent of our Comprehension . . . it may be of use to prevail with the busy mind of man to be more cautious in meddling with things exceeding its comprehension. . . . We should not then, perhaps, be so forward, out of an affectation of an universal knowledge, to raise questions, and perplex ourselves and others with disputes, about things to which our understandings are not suited. . . . If we can . . . we may learn to content ourselves with what is attainable by us in this state.

"[Section] 5. Our Capacity Suited to our State and Concerns. . . . Men have reason to be well satisfied with what God hath thought fit for them, since he hath given them, as Saint Peter says . . . whatsoever is necessary for the convenience of life, and information of virtue; and hath put within the reach of their discovery, the comfortable provision for this life and the way that leads to a better. . . . We shall not have much reason to complain of the narrowness of our minds, if we will but employ them about *what may be of use to us;* [my italics] for of that they are very capable. . . . If we disbelieve every thing because we cannot certainly know all things, we shall do much-what as wisely as he who would not use his legs . . . because he had no wings to fly.

"[Section] 6. Knowledge of our Capacity a Cure of Scepticism and Idleness. . . . Our business here is not to know all things, but those which concern our conduct. If we can find out those measures whereby a rational creature, put in that state which man is in in this world, may and ought to govern his opinions and actions depending thereon, we need not be troubled that some other things escape our knowledge."

[71] As a loyal Catholic, Campanella accepted as final the decrees of the Roman Church.

[72] Galileo carefully avoided theological questions in his various works. For Wilkins, see the *Discourse that the Earth May Be a Planet*, London, 1640, pp. 1-2; Locke, *Essay*, I, Sections 5 and 7; Boyle, *Usefulness of Natural Philosophy, Works*, ed. Thomas Birch (6 vols.), London, 1772, II, 15 ff.

[73] Campanella, *Defense*, pp. 50, 53, and *passim;* Newton, Letter to Dr. Richard Bentley, *Works of Richard Bentley*, ed. A. Dyce (3 vols.), London,

B

Intimately associated with the rise of empirical epistemology was the development of the idea of progress. In its entirety this idea included belief in the possibility, actuality, necessity, and continuity of spiritual, artistic, intellectual, and technological improvement.[74] As a work whose objective was to prevent ecclesiastical proscription of Copernican astronomy, the *Defense of Galileo* says nothing of artistic and technological advancement,[75] and includes no unified treatment of spiritual and intellectual progress. It is apparent however from statements scattered throughout the *Defense,* as well as from its vigorous championship of man's right to investigate and to develop new ideas, that Campanella believed in the possibility, actuality, and necessity of spiritual and intellectual improvement:[76]

P. 13. Knowledge of the heavens has not as yet been perfected.
P. 19. More truth always may be discovered. . . . We are obligated to seek, for we always may learn more and thus are made a little more like God.
P. 20. The world is the book of God, and . . . we must labor upon it. . . . It is good to seek God . . . [who] always reveals new truth.

1838, III, 203 ff. Boyle bequeathed fifty pounds annually to pay for "eight sermons in the year [based on science] for proving the Christian Religion against notorious Infidels," *Works,* ed. cit., I, clxvii. The Boyle Lectures consistently sought to harmonize religion and science.

[74] Among others, the idea of progress is discussed by J.-J. Thonissen, *Quelques considérations sur la théorie du progrès indéfini,* Paris, 1860; Jules Delvaille, *Essai sur l'histoire de l'idée de progrès jusqu'à la fin du XVIIIe siècle,* Paris, 1910; J. B. Bury, *The Idea of Progress:* an inquiry into its origin and growth, London, 1920 (1921, 1924, 1928); Alfred North Whitehead, *Science and the Modern World,* New York, 1925; Ronald S. Crane, "Anglican Apologetics and the Idea of Progress, 1699-1745," *Modern Philology,* XXXI (1934), 273-306, 349-382; Pitirim A. Sorokin, *Social and Cultural Dynamics,* New York, 1937, especially II, 351-384 (Chapter X); and Robert K. Merton, *loc. cit.,* pp. 591-597. A useful supplementary study is Arthur O. Lovejoy and George Boas, *Primitivism and Related Ideas in Antiquity,* Baltimore, 1935.

[75] Campanella stresses the necessity and possibility of social, including technological progress in *The City of the Sun, passim.*

[76] There is in the *Defense* little evidence regarding Campanella's attitude toward the principle of the continuity of improvement in knowledge, according to which progress is an edifice whose parts are, can only be, and will continue to be fashioned and placed in a given sequential order. His most pertinent statement (p. 19) recognizes only an apparently non-predetermined continuity: "Copernicus . . . went back to ancient doctrines of the Pythagoreans. . . . Following him Galileo discovered new planets and new systems."

P. 25. A tiny glimmer is all we know. Therefore wisdom should
be sought in the whole book of God, which is the world, where
more truth always may be discovered.

P. 26. It is an essential part of the glory of the Christian religion
that we permit [Galileo's] method of discovering new knowledge and rectifying the old.

P. 41. The world is wisdom in material form and shows us more
as we have more capacity.

P. 53. To inquire concerning the heavens . . . is useful . . . to
enlarge our faith in immortality and in the divinity of the
human soul.

The idea of spiritual and intellectual progress advanced and
supported by Campanella is definitely related to the scientific
movement of his period, and particularly to the work of Galileo.[77]
It is also the continuation of a movement which, as Professor
Crane has recently pointed out, began before Saint Augustine
and continued through the Middle Ages.[78] Among the Fathers
and schoolmen who defended religious and intellectual progressivism was the great scholastic Thomas Aquinas, a man whose
name Campanella revered and whose work he had read with love
and care. In the *Summa Theologica* Saint Thomas declared:[79]

It seems natural to human reason to advance gradually from
the imperfect to the perfect. Hence, in the speculative sciences,
we see that the teaching of the early fathers was imperfect, and
that it was afterwards perfected by those who succeeded them.
So also in practical matters.[80]

Progress in knowledge occurs in two ways. First, on the part
of the teacher, be he one or many, who makes progress in knowledge as time goes on: and this is the kind of progress in knowledge that takes place in sciences devised by man. Secondly, on
the part of the learner; thus the master, who has perfect knowledge of the art, does not deliver it all at once to his disciple from
the very outset . . . but he condescends to the disciple's capacity
and instructs him little by little. It is in this way that men made
progress in the knowledge of faith as time went on. Hence the
Apostle (Gal. iii. 24) compares the state of the Old Testament

[77] As Campanella states in supporting such passages as those quoted
above from pp. 19-20 of the *Defense,* the idea also is related to the conception of the world as the book of God advanced by Saint Leo, Anthony,
Bernard and other Fathers.

[78] "Anglican Apologetics" . . . *loc. cit.,* pp. 274 ff.

[79] I am indebted to Professor Crane for my acquaintance with these
passages from the *Summa Theologica.*

[80] II, i, question 97, article 1 (Dominican translation).

to childhood . . . among men the knowledge of faith had to proceed from imperfection to perfection.[81]

To a limited degree, Campanella provided in the *Defense* a link in the chain which connects the Catholic theologians and the Anglican divines discussed by Professor Crane. So far as I have observed, he was in addition the first philosopher to unite in support of religious and intellectual progressivism the beliefs of medieval churchmen and the initial achievements of the modern scientific movement. Of equal historical significance is his repeated declaration that spiritual enlargement would follow inquiry into the universe of Copernicus and Galileo. In making this declaration he followed the example of the Psalmist and Prophets, as well as that of the classical writers and Fathers who had found in contemplation of the cosmos a source of religious growth and exaltation. But Campanella applied the ancient precedent to the new heavens of an heretical astronomy soon to be condemned and proscribed by the Roman Church. In so doing he marched in the vanguard of his age.[82] It was in fact not until after Newton and the *Principia* that an appreciable number of men turned consciously to the new universe for spiritual enlargement.[83]

[81] II, ii, question 1, article 7 (Dominican translation). Saint Thomas' interpretation of Galations 3. 24, which anticipates Bacon's description of earlier ages as constituting the youth of the world, is scarcely supported by the text: "Wherefore the law was our pedagogue in Christ, that we might be justified by faith."

[82] Among other pioneers was Bishop John Wilkins, chairman of the Gresham College group which became the Royal Society, one of the two first secretaries, and more than any other man the founder of the organization. In concluding his *Discourse that the Earth May Be a Planet*, London, 1640, he wrote that a penetrating search into the great universe, and the "discoveries which may be found out by a more exact inquiry" may "stir us up to behave ourselves answerably to the noble and divine nature of our souls." Continuing, he stated that "A more accurate and diligent inquiry into the nature of the celestial bodies will raise our understandings into a nearer knowledge and greater admiration of the Deity." A second English pioneer who found religious growth and exaltation in the heavens of the new astronomy was Henry More, *Democritus Platonissans*, Cambridge, 1647, *passim*. The stimulation which came to the seventeenth century from the closely related ideas of nature as a *plenum formarum* and the principle of plenitude are discussed by Professor Nicolson, "The Microscope and English Imagination," *Smith College Studies*, XVI (July, 1935), p. 70, and *passim*, and Professor Lovejoy, *The Great Chain of Being*, Harvard University Press, Cambridge, 1936.

[83] After the *Principia* of Newton had ordered and made philosophically comprehensible the heliocentric universe, and the Boyle lectures had harmonized this cosmos with religion, the practice became increasingly common in England of regarding the new heavens as a source of spiritual

C

As a prelude to discussion of Campanella's place in the seventeenth century conflict between Ancients and Moderns, it is well to recall that in the field of astronomy, the controversy was fought by groups of moderns over opposed ideas which more often than not were sired by antiquity.[84] Ancient theories of the motion of the earth were pitted against themselves and against equally ancient theories of the earth's stability.[85] Specifically, the heliocentric conception of Aristarchus, the fourth system of the world of Heraclides of Pontus, and the theory of the diurnal rotation of the central earth of Ecphantus, Nicetas, and others conflicted first one with another and secondly with the mutually antagonistic hypotheses of the Fathers, of Ptolemy, and of Vitruvius, Martianus Capella, and Barthelemy the Englishman.[86] Against the pre-Socratic conception that the Moon was earthlike and therefore corruptible, was arrayed the Aristotelian doctrine of its perfection and immutability. Nor can it be said that the "Modern" who urged heliocentric astronomy made more changes or improvements in his system than did the "Ancient" who held fast to the geocentric. Both "Ancient" and "Modern" accepted a majority of the discoveries made by the telescope.[87]

Equal confusion existed in the beliefs of individuals. Tycho Brahe accepted the heavy immovable earth of Aristotle, but rejected the Aristotelian solid orbs and immutable heavens. He utilized the planetary order of Copernicus, but attacked the indefinite cosmos of the heliocentric hypothesis and the diurnal and annual motions of the earth. Reymers, Origanus (Tost), Ridley,

growth and exaltation. Because of the proscription of heliocentric astronomy by the Roman Church, the practice developed more slowly in the continental Catholic countries.

[84] In the field of literature, the contest is accurately described as an "Ancient and Modern" controversy.

[85] The "Moderns" were well aware that they were urging modifications of ancient theories.

[86] These variant and conflicting systems, together with the opposed views of the ancients regarding the Moon and other heavenly bodies, are discussed in some detail by the present writer, "The Astronomy of *Paradise Lost*," *loc. cit.*, sections I-V; "Nicolas Reymers, and the Fourth System of the World," *loc. cit.*; and "The Seventeenth Century Doctrine of a Plurality of Words," *Annals of Science*, I (1936), 385-430.

[87] *Cf.* Marjorie H. Nicolson, "A World in the Moon," *Smith College Studies in Modern Languages*, XVII (January, 1936), No. 2.

and others accepted the Copernican planetary order and the diurnal rotation of the earth, but not its annual revolution. As Professor Richard F. Jones has pointed out, apparently the earliest advocate of the anti-Modern doctrine of the decay of nature, Francis Shakleton, was "especially interested in proving that the 'heathenish' idea of the world's being eternal, set forth by Aristotle and Galen, can be refuted by the Bible."[88] This anti-Modernist and anti-Aristotelian believed firmly with Aristotle that "the earth . . . is [in] the centre of the world."[89] Four decades later another clergyman, Godfrey Goodman, rejected the immutable and incorruptible heavens of Aristotle, and in part supported the anti-Modern and anti-Aristotelian doctrine of decay with evidence provided by the telescope of the Moderns.[90]

For the reason that the seventeenth-century conflict over astronomical theory was one which had endured for more than a millennium, and its participants were divided in and among themselves, it is superficial and perhaps misleading to describe this controversy as a battle between Ancients and Moderns. Certainly it would be inaccurate so to term the conflict discussed in the *Defense of Galileo*. Here the ancient Pythagorean hypothesis, said to be in part supported by the Fathers, advocated by Cardinal Cusanus, and developed by Copernicus and Galileo,[91] is opposed by Scriptural and theological objections to the motion of the earth and the corollary doctrine of a plurality of worlds, together with the theological dogmas founded upon the science and

---

[88] *Ancients and Moderns*, Saint Louis, 1936, pp. 24-5.
[89] *A Blazyng Starre*, London, 1580, p. 3; as quoted by Jones, *ibid.*, p. 25.
[90] *The Fall of Man*, London, 1616, pp. 378-9. Insofar as the late sixteenth and early seventeenth century doctrine of the decay of nature involved cosmology, it cannot properly be described as a part of the attack which the "Ancients" made upon the "Moderns." It is rather a symptom of the decay of the Aristotelian idea of an eternal, immutable world wherein change is confined to successive generation and corruption on the earth. As such a symptom it supports neither Ancient nor Modern, but is an indication of a period of transition from "ancient" to "modern" thought.
[91] In keeping with others of his day, Campanella does not describe accurately the astronomical beliefs of Pythagoras and Cusanus. The first left no written record. Aristotle (*De Caelo*, II, 13) says that the Pythagoreans placed fire, regarded by them as the most important element in the universe, in the center, the most important place. About this central fire revolved our earth and the antichthon, or counter-earth; then the Moon, Sun, planets, and fixed stars. Cardinal Cusanus (*De Docta Ignorantia*, II, 12) advocated only the diurnal rotation of the earth.

metaphysics of Aristotle. Other opponents included various Fathers and scholastics and the modern contemporaries who "from envy disturb themselves because of the sublime genius of Galileo," and "begrudge to others knowledge which they are ignorant of or despair to know, or because they now are called masters, are ashamed again to become disciples."[92]

As was the case in Campanella's earlier philosophical treatises, the individual most frequently censured in the *Defense* is Aristotle. The Dominican monk repeatedly attacked him as an incompetent astronomer, a handicap to science, and a menace to religion. To employ the conventional term, Campanella is in this respect quite definitely a "Modern":

Pp. 18-19. [Aristotle] makes war between God and the angels. . . . They are said to imitate him but in fact oppose him. Likewise there is war between the angels. One rushes to the east, another to the west, one to the north, a fourth to the south, and labor to move the spheres in contrary directions. Some are set to turning and an equal number to resisting. . . . He also confesses that he knows nothing of the heavens and did not take pains to learn the science of astronomy. . . . I pass over the impieties which follow his doctrine of the fifth essence and eternal motion of the heavens.

P. 24. [They] enchain the intellect by human capacity . . . whoever would place us in the shackles of Aristotle, Ptolemy, and such others.

P. 25. It is a marvel . . . that the heathen not only are taken for masters, but as masters of the theologians.

P. 48. Do we not therefore condemn all Fathers of ignorance and impiety when we permit the impossible, the contradictory and the false by defending Aristotle and placing him in the Cathedral of Christ above holy teachers?

Not only did Campanella censure Aristotle and the Aristotelians, but he castigated the contemporaries who believe "God no longer creates men of excellent natural capacities."[93] He revered Plato and did not regard the "Christian" as intrinsically his equal. Nevertheless Campanella believed "natural qualities are born in us as well as in Plato . . . and because the Christian possesses the Gospel, he has the power to advance beyond Plato."[94] The

---

[92] P. 31.   [93] P. 24.
[94] P. 20. Campanella went so far as to cite Plato against contemporary advocates of the superiority of the ancients.

true "Modern" that he was, the Dominican monk was convinced that the "ancient philosophers do not excel in natural philosophy and astronomy."[95]

V

Reaction to the *Defense of Galileo* seems to have followed immediately upon its publication in 1622. Before a year had passed, Marin Mersenne had challenged the assertion of Campanella that despite the evidence of sensory observation Catholic theologians swore by the word of and followed only Aristotle. Mersenne included other anti-Aristotelians, but his reply is pointed directly toward the arguments advanced by Campanella, whose name is the first to be mentioned.[96] A decade later the *Defense* was commented upon and censured by Robert Burton in his frequently republished *Anatomy of Melancholy*,[97] and in 1658 was attacked in passing by Elias Ashmole, founder of the museum which bears his name.[98] In contrast with the censure of Mersenne, Burton, and Ashmole is the cordial welcome given the *Defense* by two of the most important intellectual and social leaders of the seventeenth century, Bishop John Amos Comenius (Komenski) and Bishop John Wilkins. Not only did these influential liberals praise Campanella but they definitely were influenced by him. In the preface to one of his earliest books, *Physicae ad Lumen Divinum reformatae Synopsis,* Comenius declared:[99]

But it happened that a certain learned man, to whom I communicated these complaints of mine [regarding the need "for the repairing of philosophy"] in a more familiar manner, shewed me a Book called *Prodromus philosophiae instaurandae* by Thomas Campanella an Italian; which I read over with incredible joy, and being inflamed with an exceeding great hope of new light, I greedily turned through his *Realis philosophia epilogistica* . . . set forth in four books, as also the books *de rerum sensu,* wherever I could get them. Whereby I found my desires in some sort satisfied, but not throughout.[100]

[96] P. 21.
[96] *Questiones Celeberrimae in Genesim,* Paris, 1623, Preface.
[97] II, iii, 2, "Air Rectified" (London, 1898, p. 326).
[98] *The Way to Bliss,* London, 1658, p. 13.
[99] Leipzig, 1633; Amsterdam, 1643. An English translation was published, London, 1651, under the title *Natural Philosophie Reformed by Divine Light: or A Synopsis of Physicks.* I quote a partially modernized text of this translation.
[100] *Synopsis,* sig. [5] recto and verso. Comenius has just concluded discussion of Ludovicus Vives, who "saw better what was not than what was."

Subsequent to a brief comment on the *"Apology* for Gali-
laeus," Comenius stated that sometime afterwards he met with
Bacon's *"Instauratio magna,* an admirable work, and which I look
upon . . . as a most bright beam of a new age of philosophers
now arising. . . . Yet it grieved me again, that I saw most noble
Verulam present us indeed with a true key of nature, but not
open the secrets of nature, only shewing us by a few examples
how they were to be opened."[101] As he continued, Comenius wrote
that despite the flaws he had found in Campanella and Bacon, "I
saw nevertheless that my hopes were not quite left in suspense,
in as much as I perceived my mind so enlightened by the light
which it received from those several sparks [that it had] now
grown wellnigh to a torch, [and] that some great secrets of nature
and very obscure places of Scripture . . . were now plain."[102]
Throughout the remainder of his preface, Comenius continued to
praise both Campanella and Bacon, but his indebtedness to the
Dominican monk is apparently somewhat greater than that to
the Lord Chancellor:[103]

For now with those [Vives?, Campanella and Bacon] that
have lighted upon a more sound way of philosophy in this age,
I saw and rested in it: 1. That the only true, genuine and plain
way of philosophy is to fetch all things from sense, reason and
Scripture. . . . And for the first we make three principles of
philosophy, with Campanella, and his . . . Sense, Reason, and
Scripture. . . . For did not God bring man into the School of
the World to contemplate his manifold Wisdom? Did not he
command him to behold his invisible things by these things that
are seen? . . . Aristotle is not to be tolerated in Christian schools,
as the only Master of philosophy . . . we should be free philosophers to follow that which our senses, reason, and Scripture dictate. . . . Why do we not, I say, turn over the living book of

[101] *Ibid.,* sig. [6] recto.   [102] *Ibid.,* sig [6] verso.
[103] I quote Comenius at some length in part for the reason that it is
not uncommon to emphasize the influence which Bacon had upon him at
the expense of that which proceeded from Campanella. Professor S. S.
Laurie (*John Amos Comenius,* Cambridge, 1904, pp. 69 ff.) discusses the
influence of both men but ignores the significant verbal indebtedness to
Campanella, the "we make three principles of philosophy, with Campanella,"
and at the least leaves the impression that Bacon affected Comenius much
more than did the Dominican monk. Doubtless for the reason that he is
primarily interested in English writers, Professor Jones (*op. cit.,* pp. 137-8)
ignores Campanella in his discussion of the *Synopsis,* and concludes with
the statement that "Comenius's significance lies in his appreciation of the
progressive thinkers of his age, especially Bacon." . . .

the world instead of dead books? wherein we may contemplate more things, and with greater delight and profit than any one can tell us. . . . Now he that will may see Campanella and Verulamius, for it may suffice to have shewed these Hercules, who have happily put their hands to the subduing of Monsters and cleansing Augias's stables. . . . Aristotle with all his heathenish train should be excluded from the sacred Philosophy of Christians. . . . And indeed the most sad estate of the Church a little after shews what fruit we had in coupling Aristotle with Christ, when . . . heresy sprung out of heresy. . . . Where in forging articles of faith, and ordaining rules of life, Aristotle had an equal share with Christ, if I may not say he had the sole dictatorship, of which thing our School divinity will give us a very clear sight.[104]

As the reader of the *Defense* will observe, the lines last quoted from Comenius frequently echo its passages. I may mention however that Comenius's contention that the authority of Aristotle should not be permitted in Christian schools suggests the rhetorical question which opens the *Defense*: "Is it allowable and desirable to suppress both the Aristotelian sect and the authority of heathen philosophers, and for Christian schools to teach the new philosophy?" Where Campanella urged study of the book of the world rather than the little books of men, Comenius asked why we do not scan the living book of the world rather than dead books. Both writers stress the points that Aristotle was a heathen who occasioned heresies, and that he has been made the teacher of Christians.

The indebtedness of Bishop Wilkins to the *Defense* is equally fundamental, and includes much more extensive verbal borrowing.[105] An appreciable portion of the content and to an important degree the major themes of both *Discovery* and *Discourse* were drawn from Campanella's work. Virtually a third of the subject-matter of the second proposition (chapter) of the *Discovery*, "That a plurality of worlds doth not contradict any principle of reason or faith," is adapted from the *Defense*. Both *Discovery* and *Discourse* redeem nobly the failure which Campanella called the greatest sin of his day, that "we have neither made known

[104] *Synopsis,* sigs. [6] verso ff. I have not included a half dozen passages equally close to Campanella's statements in the *Defense.*
[105] I discuss Wilkins's use of the *Defense* in some detail in "The Debt of Bishop John Wilkins to the *Apologia pro Galileo.*"

the new earths, the new systems in the heavens, and the new celestial phenomena; nor declared abroad the harmony of Scripture and this kind of philosophy."[106] In his two books, the first of their kind to be published in England, the future Secretary of the Royal Society recommended to the reader but a single volume among the two hundred which he cited. The work thus honored was the *Defense of Galileo*, wherein "you may see many things worth the reading and notice."[107]

[106] *Defense*, ed. cit., p. 11.

[107] *Discovery*, London, 1640, p. 26. The following translation of the *Apologia* attempts to reproduce as faithfully as is possible in English idiom the flavor and spirit as well as the meaning of the original. Extended paragraphs and highly complex sentences not infrequently have been divided, the ever-present emphatic and semi-connective adverbs reduced in number, and in a few instances, the order of sentences altered. Where the incisiveness or directness of an important statement would otherwise have been lost, unessential words have been eliminated. Conversely, words have at times been added to clarify meaning or to make it apparent without a second reading. The usual number of passages offered alternative interpretations, or seemingly required emendation. It is unnecessary to mention that the translations of Campanella's direct quotations from Scripture are those of the modern Catholic Version.

THE DEFENSE OF GALILEO,
Mathematician of Florence.

An Inquiry as to whether that Kind of Philosophy which
Galileo Has Made Famous is in Harmony with or
is Opposed to the Holy Scriptures.

By

FRIAR THOMAS CAMPANELLA,
Calabrian, of the Order of Preachers.

FRANKFORT,
Published by Gottfried Tampach;

Printed by Erasmus Kempffer.
M. DC. XXII.

The Printer to the Friendly Reader,

with best wishes for his health and peace.

Is it not futile that we little men, who live in this great world much as maggots live in a cheese, should raise fundamental questions regarding its construction? Is it not vain to ask whether the seat and dwelling-place which we call earth revolves with other globes about the Sun, or whether they and the Sun turn about our home? We are but insignificant animalcules, almost as ignorant as the rat within the ship, who, when his neighbor declared the ship and not the sea was in motion, could not determine whether their common abode moved or remained fixed upon the flowing water. Nevertheless, many learned men believe the world more worthy of minute investigation than do the uninformed. Particularly have they inquired diligently since the instrument which the Lyncean philosophers call the telescope has revealed new wonders in the globes of heaven. To be sure, some arrogant astronomers prefer to interpret and usually describe celestial things in the fashion of the vulgar. Their self-willed stupidity is not so precious that it should bar all mankind from a painstaking search after truth. There are also many theologians who desire and attempt to shackle astronomical inquiry by invoking the authority of the Holy Scriptures, but as this authority is exercised well or badly, so it is esteemed good or ill by those who love truth.

[4]

For the reason that the many distinguished men who have accepted the Copernican hypothesis were equally familiar with both Holy Scripture and the Book of the World, we cannot assume that they followed the Pythagorean forefathers either rashly, or impiously and ignorantly. In the discourse presented to you, friendly reader, this and other questions are discussed by the celebrated Italian philosopher, theologian, and monk, Thomas Campanella. Nor should you believe he is the only theologian and philosopher from this country who supports the Copernican hypothesis. Had Paolo Antonio Foscarini written the work in Latin, so that it properly might serve as an appendix to the present book, you would read subsequent to the treatise by Campanella the courageous *Epistle* of this Carmelite monk, addressed by him to Sebastiano Fantoni, Italian General of the Order, and printed in Naples, 1615, by Lazzaro Scoriggio. In this noble epistle Foscarini defends the new Pythagorean system of the world, including the Pythagorean and Copernican theory of the motion of the earth and the stability of the Sun.

The considered and reasoned arguments of Campanella and Foscarini complement those set forth by the Germans, Nicolas, Cardinal of Cusa, Nicolas Copernicus, Georg Joachim Rheticus, Michael Maestlin and David Origanus; the Italians, Giordano Bruno, of Nola, Francesco Patrizio, Galileo Galilei and Redento Baranzano; the Englishmen, William Gilbert and Nicolas Hill, and especially those now advanced by our own John Kepler. In keeping with others among the many philosophers who became Copernicans immediately following the *Starry Messenger* of Galileo, I venture to assert, and have no doubt, friendly reader, but that he who judges this hypothesis soon will be more favorable to it. Farewell, and in future days expect additional discourses from Campanella.

[5]

To the Most Illustrious, Esteemed, and Venerable
Boniface Cardinal Gaetani,
Friar Thomas Campanella
Wishes Health and Peace.

Behold, I send you, Venerable Master, an inquiry—carefully
wrought with your permission—where I discuss in their relation
to Sacred Scripture the motion of the earth, the stability of the
sphere of the stars, and arguments supporting the Copernican
system. You will know what is rightly said, and what should be
rejected or strengthened, because you have this power by man-
date of the Holy Senate. I submit my judgment not only to the
Holy Church, and to all superior wisdom, but principally to you,
great patron of Italian muses. Their patron living, they shall not
perish. May you therefore live eternally. Amen.

THE DEFENSE OF GALILEO

FOREWORD

It is now essential to discuss two questions: first, should the
new philosophy be permitted to search for truth, and secondly,
is it desirable or allowable to suppress both the Aristotelian sect
and the authority of heathen philosophers, and for our Christian
schools to teach the new philosophy in harmony with Sacred Doctrine? A third fundamental controversy has been precipitated by
those who condemn the exalted philosophy of Galileo the Florentine because they believe it opposed to the dogmas of Holy Scripture. I shall reply as the truth appears to me.

. . . .

I ask therefore: Is the philosophy which Galileo has made
famous and important in harmony with or opposed to the Holy
Scriptures? Five chapters will complete this inquiry. In the first
I shall set forth the arguments and contentions which oppose
Galileo; in the second, those which support him. I shall develop
in the following chapter three hypotheses which lead to a double
conclusion, and answer in the fourth the arguments brought
against Galileo. In the fifth and last I shall discuss [and in part
refute] the arguments which favor him.

said and as I say in *Anti-Machiavelli,* such hypocrisy is a lethal disease of the soul.

I turn now to the second requirement for men who would sit as judges in questions which involve religion. Unless they have received explicit revelation from God, those who have only the love of God and not knowledge, are incompetent to decide these questions. That they are most saintly is of no avail. In Romans 10 the Apostle censured the efforts of the Jews, because they attempted to become Christians by means of a zeal for God, but not according to knowledge. Indeed, he says that he once believed indulgence in zeal distinguished him in the eyes of God. He was erudite, and had learned both law and secular doctrine at the feet of Gamaliel, but found he had not properly examined all arguments of the Christian faith. [In 1. Timothy, 1.13] he exclaimed, [I obtained mercy, because] I did it ignorantly in unbelief. It was the love of God and of the word of Scripture which moved holy and learned Lactantius and Augustine to deny the existence of antipodes. They argued that inhabited antipodes are contrary to Scripture, because neither the men said to live there nor their ancestors could have crossed the impassable ocean and for this reason could not be sons of Adam. Other Fathers denied antipodes because they held Christ would of necessity be crucified both here and there, or for the reason advanced by Justin that heaven is shaped as a vault. The base of this vault is the earth; above are the waters, and above the waters the immobile heaven. [13]

We have since learned that such reasoning is false. It arose from defective mathematics and cosmography, and resulted in distortion of the meaning of Scripture. The belief of Saint Thomas that men could not live on the equator likewise was proved untrue. This error developed in part from incomplete knowledge of geography and physiology, and in part from a passion for Aristotle, whose words Saint Thomas preferred to accept rather than the evidence of Albertus Magnus and Avicenna. Because they could not understand how the four rivers and the many great trees of the earthly paradise could exist except in an immense space, a zeal for Scripture led Saint Ephrem,

Anastasius of Sinai, and Moses, Bishop of Syria, to place this paradise in the opposite hemisphere. The testimony of sailors shows that they also were deceived. We are correct when we say that without knowledge holy men cannot judge rightly. Indeed, it was because of this fact that in his *Reply* to impugners of the religious orders, chapter 11, Saint Thomas chose the gloss on Daniel 1 when he censured their ridicule of the study of philosophy: "What if the man ignorant of mathematics should attack mathematics, or lacking philosophy, should attack philosophy? Who does not scorn to be laughed at by such mockers?" The comic poet [Terence] said of such a judge:

Immortal Gods, no man is more unjust than he who lacks knowledge;
He considers nothing right except what he has done himself.

THE SECOND HYPOTHESIS

There are six things which the judge should know if he is to be prepared to judge correctly:

(1) The philosophic theologian requires a knowledge of mundane and celestial phenomena for the refutation of sectarians.

(2) Knowledge of the heavens has not as yet been perfected by astronomers.

(3) The holy Moses and our Lord Jesus Christ provided us with spiritual doctrine not to be had from nature, and taught us the way to live happily. They did not seek to reveal astronomy or natural philosophy, for "God left the world to the disputes of men," Ecclesiastes 3, and "the invisible things of God are clearly understood from the things that are made," Romans 1.

(4) That which forbids Christians the study of philosophy and search for knowledge likewise forbids them to be Christians. [14] Because they need not fear what is false, the law of the Christians commends all knowledge to them.

(5) The enemies of Galileo attack philosophers who so much as examine the dogmas of Christian doctrine by reason and experiment, although no text is expounded and nothing is concluded which is expressly opposed to Holy Scripture. Their conduct works perniciously against themselves, impiously against the

faith, and with mockery against others. It is much more desirable to harmonize one interpretation of Scripture with philosophy when the other is discordant.

(6) Although it may have been regarded as heresy in the militant church, as it perhaps is in the church triumphant, not all that is false is injurious to Scripture. It must directly or indirectly destroy the true meaning. In addition, if a theologian has advanced doctrines which apparently are equally or more opposed to Holy Scripture than are the theories of Galileo, he is neither condemned nor prohibited from making further inquiry. It is by such inquiry that he determines whether the doctrines advanced are sound. He does not impugn faith, but rather opens truth to the soul.

Without burdensome repetition, and in so far as it is useful for understanding the question at issue, I shall examine these six statements in the light of matters which pertain to our theology.

EXAMINATION OF THE FIRST ASSERTION

As Saint Thomas teaches in the *Summa Theologica,* II, ii, questions 8 and 9, and all other theologians, it is sufficient for the Christian that he know those beliefs which are necessary for his eternal salvation. But this knowledge is inadequate for the theologian who must overcome opposition and lead others to sound doctrine. So says the Apostle, and with him the Fathers. The theologian also must know all things by the highest Cause, which is God, and not by lower causes, in the manner of the ingenious and the shrewd. He is required to know thoroughly all sciences, as well as God—his principal end—and to understand all the work of God. If the knowledge which proceeds from ideas concerning God and the works of God among men is believed to contradict divine knowledge, he must be prepared to reply with argument. Truth does not contradict truth, nor the effect its cause. We were admonished by the Lateran Council under Leo X that human knowledge does not oppose the divine, or the works of God contradict God.

In his *Reply* to those who cavilled because [15] the Friars studied eloquence and secular knowledge, Saint Thomas showed the critics to be blind and unable to see how necessary, if not how useful, knowledge is to the theologian. Theology itself requires no demonstration from human knowledge, but there is need we should be strengthened by comprehending the supernatural from natural and sensible things. The necessity of this is shown by the statements of Augustine, Jerome, Dionysius, and the other Fathers who both learned from and taught men to learn from nature. Jerome declared in the *Epistle to Magnus,* "You do not know what you should first admire in these people, their secular erudition or knowledge of Scripture." The Apostle read and often quoted the poets and philosophers. When Gregory expounds in his *Moral*s the passage in Job, "Who maketh Arcturus and Orion," he praises the wisdom which is obtained from secular astronomers. The Fathers held the same opinion, and Saint Thomas says in the *Summa Theologica,* I, question 1, article 5, where he discusses the related passage from Solomon, that wisdom, or theology, called her handmaids, the sciences, to the tower.

It is clear that all sciences, not this or that particular science, were born in man. God made man that he might know God, and knowing, love God, and loving, might enjoy him. He therefore created man rational and with senses. If our mind is capable of receiving knowledge, man transgresses the natural law of God if he does not use this gift from the divine plan of God. In the common phrase, Chrysostom does not desire to walk with his feet. Aristotle declared that all men wish to know nature, and Moses said in Genesis 2: "The Lord God took man and put him into the paradise of pleasure, to dress it and keep it." All the animals obeyed him, and without cultivation all things flourished by spontaneous growth, so that his labor was neither the tilling of soil nor the custody of animals. His work was rather to speculate upon things, and because of wonder to observe the heavens and nature. Since he revered God he gave himself to philosophy, for as the Apostle says, we cannot know without previous reflection that the invisible things of God are clearly observed in the things that are made. Because Adam yet lacked experience, all learning was poured into him. Yet, as the Fathers testify, this instruction was not given him as an individual, but as the head of the human race, and for the benefit of us who have descended from him.

David advises us, "Seek God, and your soul lives." God cannot be sought by us except in natural things created by him, for the cause is sought in the effects. He sings elsewhere, "Wonderful is thy work, and therefore my soul hath searched." Having investigated with care all things under the Sun, Solomon highly praised comprehensive knowledge in Ecclesiastes 1, and declared in Wisdom 7 he had known all natural things, including mathematics, astronomy, and logic. [16] As his hearers desired, he discussed in 3 [1] Kings 4 the whole of the physical realm, and spoke of plants and birds, of stones and of fish. From the beginning the world was called the wisdom of God (as was revealed to Saint Brigid), and a book in which we may read all things. Therefore Saint Leo says in his seventh discourse, "We receive signs of the divine will as much in the elementary world as in the revealed pages." He likewise proves this truth in the eighth discourse from the passages, "The heavens show forth the glory of God" *et cetera,* and "The invisible things of God are clearly seen from the things that are made." And indeed, as Cyril writes in the first treatise against Julian, "philosophy is the catechism of faith," and destroys that which is opposed to faith. Bernard says in a further discourse, "I shall hear what the Lord declares to me: the world is the book of God, in which we should read continually." Nicephorus testifies Saint Anthony believed the same, and so did Chrysostom when he expounded the passage in Psalm 147, "God hath not done in like manner to every nation." No one can be pardoned who rejects the law that he search. Truly, "From all the earth went forth their sound."

Corollary. Because the things which are most marvellous and excellent represent more completely their author God, and because their study confirms the divinity of the human soul, they are studied with the greater devotion. Among these things are the heavens and the stars, and the great systems of the world. Therefore Anaxagoras said man was made that he might view the heavens, and all theologians, particularly Lactantius, praised Ovid for his lines:

> Though all other animals are prone, and gaze upon the earth,
> God gave to man an upright face, and bade
> Him stand erect and turn his eyes to heaven.

In Psalm 18 David sings, "The heavens show forth the glory of God, and the Firmament declareth the work of his hands," and in Psalm 8, "For I will behold thy heavens, the works of thy fingers; the moon and the stars which thou hast founded." In *Epinomis* and in *Axiochus* (if perhaps it is not by Xenophon), Plato demonstrated the immortality of the soul and the dignity and divinity of man from knowledge of the stars, equinoxes, eclipses and similar phenomena of the heavens. This we prove further in *Anti-Machiavelli*. Ovid declared when he wrote of astronomers:

> Oh happy souls that first took thought
> To know these things and scale the skies above; [. . .]
> [17] They brought the distant stars into our ken
> And heaven itself subjected to their skill.

As I plainly state elsewhere, the praise given astronomy by these writers supports completely the work of Galileo. I shall not add what Josephus and Philo inform us regarding the value of physical and astronomical knowledge, and what Berosus in his work on Noah and Abraham observes concerning this family. Scripture shows that by means of physiology the Patriarch Jacob effected a division of the flocks and liberated himself from Laban's avarice. Because of their knowledge, the ancient fathers were long-lived. Moreover, God placed the first sign of Christ's coming in heaven and earth. "Yet one little while, and I will move the heaven and the earth, [. . .] and the desired of all nations shall come," he prophesied in Aggeus (Haggai). By means of eccentrics, equinoxes, and apogees then beginning mutation and now finally brought forth, we show in another work that a sign appeared.

That there shall be signs in Sun and Moon and stars is clearly affirmed by the Evangelist in Luke 21. But ancient astronomers were unable to ascertain the cause of the sign which foretold

Christ's coming, and events transpired as the Apostle Peter prophesied in *Epistle* 2, third chapter: "There shall come deceitful scoffers" (as the Aristotelians and Machiavellians), "walking after their own lusts and saying, Where is his promise or his coming? for since the time that the fathers slept, all things continue as they were from the beginning of the creation." I show however that all things did not continue as they were at the beginning, and that signs appeared in Sun and Moon and stars. In his treatise on Luke 21 Saint Gregory demonstrates accurately by arguments based on the absence of change in the mundane world that these events occurred near to the day of Christ.

Those who prohibit diligent observation of the phenomena and changes of heaven desire that the Day of the Lord shall come upon us either as a thief in the night or as other sons of darkness. Saint Paul so teaches regarding this Day in 1 Thessalonians 5, and warns us to watch and be not children of night. He truly watches who observes signs which appear in Sun and Moon and stars. He does not who follows the ancient Jews in despising signs, as did Balaam when he encountered the offending stone. We therefore before all others believe with the Apostles in the writings of the first book of nature. Because of these things David said, "From all the earth goes forth their sound, and are not words" *et cetera,* and Paul repeated this truth in Romans 1. The Books of God harmonize one with the other.

EXAMINATION OF THE SECOND ASSERTION

No philosopher or theologian has yet formulated a wholly desirable or satisfactory hypothesis of the arrangement of the universe, or of the nature, order, situation, quantity, motion, and configuration of the heavens. [18] Nor is such an hypothesis possible, as is shown both by the diversity of theories among learned astronomers and by the words of Sacred Scripture. It is said in Job 38, "Dost thou know the order of heaven, and canst thou set down the reason thereof on the earth?" and a few verses below, "Who can declare the order of the heavens?" Solomon wrote thereafter in Ecclesiastes 9, "God hath delivered the world to their consideration, so that man cannot find out the work which God hath made from the beginning to the end," and repeated this and similar thoughts in chapter 8.

They are therefore mad who believe that Aristotle constructed the true system of the heavens, and that further inquiry should not be made. Aristotle repeats in 2 *De Caelo* only what he had learned from the Egyptians: there are eight spheres, numbered stars, and the primum mobile. In twenty-four hours this primum mobile turns all the planetary spheres with violent motion from east to west, but at the same time the spheres are carried by their natural motion a short distance from west to east. The Moon, for example, is whirled by all the spheres in a violent daily revolution while it moves in the opposite direction approximately twelve of three hundred and sixty degrees. In 12 *Metaphysics* however, the spheres are not hurried along by the primum mobile, but each one is moved by an angelic intelligence. Thus Aristotle multiplies intelligences, which in truth are only appearances and motion. Nor does he provide reasons for these appearances, as Saint Thomas, Simplicius, and other commentators confess. He makes war between God and the angels by causing them to move contrary to his motion. They are said to imitate God, but in fact they oppose him. Likewise there is war between the angels. One angel rushes to the east, another to the west, one to the north, a fourth to the south, and labor to move the spheres in contrary directions. Some are set to turning and an equal number to resisting. In this way Aristotle brings violence into heaven and discord or weariness among the angels.

For what purpose are the stars at one time seen hastening forward, and at another to be moved a greater distance backward? To what end are the planets made stationary, swift-moving, retrograde, and slow? Aristotle gives no reason, nor is he able to give a reason for changes in eccentricity and of apogees and equinoxes, or why he compounds heaven of the fifth essence. Because of what purpose is acronychus Mars seen to descend below the sphere of the Sun, and according to his philosophy how can there exist spots on the Sun, the new star in the eighth sphere, and comets above the Moon? All his astronomy is false, and both instruments and the senses prove with certainty that it cannot be accepted. In fact, Saints Basil and Ambrose regarded as heretics those who joined Aristotle in constructing heaven from the fifth essence, and in denying that the Sun is actually composed of heat. These things I discuss below, and prove in my *Sacred Philosophy.* [19] I omit that Aristotle places the Sun immediately above the Moon, a belief which Saint Thomas and all followers of the Stagirite teach is false. He confesses he knew nothing of the heavens, and did not take pains to learn the science of Astronomy. This situation he makes obvious in 12 *Metaphysics,* where he acknowledges that he drew upon Calippus and Eudoxus, and contributed only additional revolving orbs—the orbs which intensify the battles between the angels. I also pass over the impieties which follow his doctrine of the fifth essence and of the eternal motion of the heavens. Saint Thomas and the Christian commentators have made these apparent. Moreover, Saint Thomas teaches in chapter 10, *De Coelo,* that the doctrine of an actual and not of a theoretical eternal motion excludes the existence of God. Aristotle would make us atheists who deny eternal motion, but Saint Thomas refuted him. I cannot marvel enough at those theologasters who limit the genius of men by the writings of Aristotle.

The new celestial phenomena declare that Aristotle and Ptolemy did not attain truth. Their doctrine explains neither these phenomena nor the discord in the heavens. I omit the errors in mathematics detected by Copernicus, such as that which produced regular motion in one sphere moving on the center of another, and to avoid which Thebit and King Alfonso invented librations and a ninth sphere. But Copernicus pointed out that these additions are deceptions and turned back to the ancient doctrines of the Pythagoreans, where better explanations of the phenomena are presented. Following him, Galileo discovered new planets and new systems, and unknown changes in heaven. How ignorant and senseless they are, who consider satisfactory the theories of the heavens set forth by Aristotle. He entreated other men to investigate, and as he himself confessed, advanced no doctrines truly his own. His uncertain followers now fiercely dispute.

Appendix. What may be said? If it is not possible to obtain a theory of the heavens which is sound and authoritative, it is preferable, as Job suggests, to remain quiescent and not search in vain. This I admit, but question the point that astronomical inquiry makes men heretics, although perhaps it makes them vain. But I shall investigate further what is not vain—the natural longing which teaches us more truth always may be discovered. Saint Bernard wrote in his *Manual* for Eugene, "Although God is not to be discovered, it is most rewarding always to seek." When we inquire concerning celestial things, we inquire of God, for whom we are commanded ever to search. Paul admonished the Athenians that we are obligated to seek, for we always may learn more and thus are made a little more like God. [20] Aristotle himself says in 1 *De Anima* that it is better to know probably a few great things than many small ones demonstratively. Therefore the Chaldeans, and subsequently, many Egyptians studied the heavens; later, many Greeks, and now many Germans and Italians. We are amazed by the magnificent scene which Galileo unfolds, in which the God of wisdom and power and love brings forth his riches.

Saint Leo, Anthony, Bernard, Chrysostom, and other Fathers declare that the world is the book of God and that we must labor upon it. In the discourse where Bernard reprimands the search for God in supernatural things, he teaches that God is found in those which are natural, and that by these things we are raised to him. Richard of St. Victor sets forth lucidly this belief in the discourse on contemplation found in the books on Benjamin. Reason also approves it. If God created the world because of his glory, as Solomon says, he indeed wills that in his creation we should admire, praise, and celebrate the author. Truly, the wise poet and painter desire that their poems and pictures be seen, and having been seen, that the excellency of the art be known, and the artist praised. We have said that by such inquiry, divinity of soul is strengthened and displayed. It cannot be vain to search.

Those who believe the summation of all things is found in Aristotle and other ancient philosophers drive out faith in God. They are jealous by nature and forbid man a widening search, especially after the light of the Gospels and newly discovered orbs and stars the ancients knew not of. They cloud the light of faith which raises us above the heathen and does not bow to their yoke. Cyril testifies that philosophy is the perfect doctrine and catechism of religious things. If we neglect not the love that is in us, we are able better to read from the world, the book and the wisdom of God. This I say holds for the pages yet unturned. It is not that I elevate the simple nature of the Christian to equality with the nature of Plato. But natural qualities are born in us as well as in Plato and others, and because the Christian possesses Scripture he has the power to advance in knowledge beyond Plato and any other. Plato himself said that men born in the present age only give place to the ancients because their contemporaries venerate the dead and envy the living. To continue, the point again is proved by the saying of Jeremiah that it is good to seek God. Saint Bernard declared and we noted above that God always reveals new truth. If you suppress the new truth, you cannot receive the old. It is not vain to search continually. In the words of Saint Leo, "He who thinks himself to have achieved does not achieve, unless he abandon all in the search for Divinity."

[21]   EXAMINATION OF THE THIRD ASSERTION

I have shown that the ancient philosophers do not excel in natural philosophy and astronomy, and now shall demonstrate that neither Christ nor Moses prescribed bounds for these sciences. Christ is never interpreted in the Gospel as discussing physics or astronomy, but rather morals and promises of eternal life—the way of which he set forth by example, by doctrine, and by his blood. Indeed, such discussion had been superfluous. In the beginning God left the world to the disputes of men, while they labored and learned of God by the things he had made. He gave us a rational mind so that we might inquire, and as Saint Clement interprets the Apostle Peter, he disclosed methods of investigation by the five senses. These are as windows through which man beholds the world, the image of God. As Chrysostom

on Psalm 147 and others declare, man then admires what is
found in it, and seeks God the artist.

All theologians believe we did not lose by original sin the
natural powers of our senses. It therefore would have been superfluous for him who comes to redeem us from sin to teach a
second time what we should discern and are able to discern for
ourselves. He did not command the Apostles to instruct us in
natural things, but to baptize and to teach the things which he
performed and taught (Matthew 28) ; and to demonstrate them
by miracle and martyrdom (Mark 16). Bernard informs us in
his discourse on Peter and Paul that "the apostles did not teach
men the art of fishing or tent-making, nor to uncover the subtlety
of Aristotle, nor to read Plato, nor any specific thing; but taught
them the living Christ." Saint Clement says in I *Recognitions*
that when the Roman philosophers asked of Barnabus, Why did
nature give the little gnat six feet and the great elephant only
four? he replied that Christ commanded him to teach the doctrine
of the kingdom of heaven, not the phenomena which can be discovered by natural means. Nor did the Apostles condemn philosophy, but recounted that Christ indirectly commended the Pharisees because they foretold rain and calm by the appearance of
heaven. To be sure, he rebuked them because they did not know
by the same method the time of the Messiah written in the signs.
The signs of heaven also are described as carefully sought after
in Jeremiah 10.

It is well known that Moses does not prescribe bounds to
human knowledge, and that God did not instruct him in either
natural science or astronomy. Solomon says that God left the
world to the disputes of men, [22] and that he himself diligently
investigated all things. Nor did he read from the book of Moses
but rather from nature. Indeed, when Moses spoke of heaven and
earth and of all things in the creation, he described their superficial aspects, and as they serve the lawgiver rather than the
philosopher. In the same fashion he depicted God as the creator
and governor of the world who gave the law. He began with
creation, proceeded to government, and went thereafter to the
particular type of law which he announced. Such an interpreta-

tion is presented by all the Fathers, who add that he followed the popular manner of speech and addressed more the physical senses of the people than the intellects of philosophers. Since Moses was unusually learned in every field of knowledge, both divine and human, he inspired all the wisdom of the Egyptians. This is stated in Acts 7, and proved by Philo and Josephus. Because of his manner of speech he satisfied the people, and by his knowledge contented the philosophers. He made the latter understand all things not only by words but also by deeds. They interpreted the deeds mystically, as we observe in the construction of the tabernacle similar to heaven, the robe of Aaron covering the whole sphere of the earth, candelabra about the seven planets, the great marvels of the Fathers, and the statements of Solomon in Wisdom 18, of Paul in Hebrews, and of the Rabbis.

Because of the prevalent belief that Scripture contained a mystical meaning for the wise as well as an obvious meaning for the vulgar, the learned understood that when God said in creating heaven, "Be light made," the light was the angels. With Augustine and other Fathers, the six days which Moses describes do not refer to the physical but to the angelic creation. For the reason that the vulgar worshipped physical idols and could neither understand nor adore incorporeal and spiritual beings, Augustine and Chrysostom teach that Moses included no description of the creation of the angels. He also did not inform the people of the kind of material employed in the creation of the world, but the wise regard this as water and earth. Saint Thomas says in the *Summa Theologica,* I, question 68, article 3, that he did not mention air because he desired to set forth nothing unknown to the rude people. It was unknown to them whether the invisible air is a body or an appearance produced by shadows of the abyss above.

All Fathers who discuss the text of Moses in connection with philosophy unanimously make allowance for his method of accommodating his books to the capacity of the people. In his allegories on Moses, Bishop Anastasius demonstrated that he gave important place to figurative expression. To be sure, the greatest champion of the wisdom of Moses, Saint Chrysostom, opposed stoutly allegorical interpretation and reduced the entire text to literal statement of meaning and moral instruction. Nevertheless, he acknowledged that Moses accommodated his words to the vulgar, particularly in the passage, "God made two great lights." [23] The Moon indeed is smaller than both the earth and many of the stars, but the words *greater light* were used because to the senses the Moon appears larger than the stars. Saint Thomas likewise proves in *Summa Theologica,* I, question 70, article 1, that here and in other passages Moses followed the common manner of speech. He did not however imitate the vulgar in his reason, for this makes the Moon the smaller light. Moses also followed the vulgar when he described the stars and the motion of heaven. Neither the motion of the sphere itself nor that of the lights within it is obvious to the senses, so that Moses did not speak of the stars as moving. If the opinion of Aristotle were true, and he spoke literally, he would describe them as in motion. (See my response to this third and to the fifth assertions.) As I shall point out in the fifth assertion, he is ridiculous and stupidly irreligious who seeks to condemn astronomers because they declare the Moon is smaller than many stars, is no larger than a third part of the earth, and shines with reflected light, only because Moses calls the Moon a great light.

EXAMINATION OF THE FOURTH ASSERTION

Every law or doctrine of mankind which forbids its followers to investigate natural things should be suspected of falsehood. Truth certainly does not contradict truth, as the Lateran Council under Leo X and others declared. Nor does the created book of God's wisdom contradict the revealed book of his divine wisdom. Whosoever fears opposition from natural phenomena is but conscious of his own falseness. We all acknowlege that the Mohammedans proscribe science for this reason. When the Moors studied philosophy many of them attacked the Mohammedan faith, including Averroes, Avicenna, Alfarabius, Haly, Albenragel, Albumasar, and other philosophers and astronomers. This I prove in *Anti-Machiavelli,* and Boterus relates that because of these philosophers the Moorish King prohibited all science. The Sultans of Turkey protected their faith in this fashion, and the unbelieving Gentiles established the law that inquisitive search should not be made concerning the gods. Because of this legal prohibition Plato advises us in the *Timaeus* that we speak of the gods in the fashion which the lawmakers, and the gods, desire. He himself wished to have only one God for his countersign. When Chrysostom commented on the Epistle to the Romans, he condemned Socrates because he knew the falseness of belief in many gods and yet said when dying, we are indebted to the priests of Gallus for Æsculapius. (See Plato in *Phaedo* regarding this statement by Socrates.) The Athenians sought the death of Anaxagoras, Socrates, Aristotle, and other philosophers because they dared boldly to violate the law which prohibited inquiry concerning the gods. The Apostle testifies that the men of Athens knew the true God, as does Cato in Lucanus and many others.

They either think evil of Christianity or suspect men of evil who desire by Christian law to prohibit true knowledge, study, and inquiry concerning physical and celestial things. [24] If the Christian law is of all laws the most pregnant with truth, it contains nothing false. Not only does it fear nothing from scientific observations, but it seeks their testimony. So says Saint Thomas in his *Treatise on the Truth of the Catholic Faith Against Unbelievers,* and again in his *Reply,* or apology for the religious orders, where he refutes those who condemn in monks the study of philosophy and the sciences. In the *Summa Theologica,* I, question 1, article 5, he proves by argument and the authority of Solomon, Proverbs 9, that Wisdom or theology sends her handmaids the sciences to invite men to the tower. Because they are servants who serve truly and do not contradict, Saint Thomas does not scorn the sciences, but employs them to gather men into the Kingdom of Heaven. As we are taught by the Lateran Council, the second Council of Nicaea, and in the Articles condemned at Paris, those sciences which contradict theology are not true sciences, but are rather the vain dreams of philosophers.

That Christ approved rather than condemned knowledge is shown by the passage in 1 Corinthians 3 [1.24], where he is described as the power and the wisdom of God. Ecclesiasticus 1 declares all wisdom is from the Lord God, and the root of wisdom the word of God. Truly, the word of God is the highest reason, and by participation in it we are called rational. Christ desires that we achieve excellence, and closely resemble him in truth and works. They lessen our likeness to him when they direct us to limit our investigations by, and to believe no more than the conclusions of non-Christian men who oppose Christ. Truly, they circumscribe the work of the wisdom of God within the small brain of one man and enchain the intellect by human capacity. They do not choose to limit us by Christ. Yet it is Christ to whom Paul would subject all tyranny and wisdom, 2 Corinthians 10, and in whose shackles Ecclesiasticus places our feet.

Whosoever would place us in the shackles of Aristotle, Ptolemy, or such others as the Averroists (by whom Antonio Mirandola is not untainted), and think their dogmas enslave us, or that God no longer creates men of excellent natural capacities, truly, such men are not Christians. They declare the words of God are superior to the testimony of nature, the book of God, and torture the meaning of Scripture to fit their limited interpretations. The wisdom of God is exceedingly vast, and is not the narrow capacity of one man. As much more as is sought, so much more is discovered in Deity. We openly admit that we know nothing when we are willing to ignore so much and so many things in nature. Solomon ponders over natural knowledge in Ecclesiastes, the Apostle commends it, and Socrates skilled himself in it. [25] Those who think they are informed because they know Aristotle, or as Galileo, because they have discovered new phenomena in the world, the book of God, do not know the manner in which they must know, unless they know much more than they are ignorant of. Nor are they truly wise who, as if they knew, desist from inquiry, unless they know more than they do not know. So say Saint Leo and Ecclesiasticus 42 and 43. Indeed, a tiny glimmer is all that we know. Therefore wisdom should be sought in the whole book of God, which is the world, where more wisdom always may be discovered. It is to this book and not to the little books of men that Scripture sends us.

We follow too frequently the doctrines of the heathen, for rational conceptions came first from the reason of Christ. To the

extent that men reject superstition, they partake in Christ and
his reason. When those who are superstitious discuss what is
good, it is well, says Augustine in 2 *The Christian Doctrine,* to
withdraw from them as we withdraw from unlawful possessors
of truth who have known but have not honored it. We were
granted faith that we might not accept superstitious beliefs. Again,
we know what is of Christ, but prefer the things that are of men.
Yet love completes nature and natural things, as Saint Thomas,
Summa Theologica, II, question 2, articles 1 ff., and the Fathers
teach. If they are equal in other ways, Christian men are better
prepared to investigate truth than are the heathen. Truly, he injures Christ who subjects himself to unbelievers. The prophet
said, "Under every leafy wood you were lying with a prostitute,"
and by this Jerome understood him to describe those who prostitute themselves to the learning and doctrine of the sectarians.
Using the figure of the Old Testament, Jerome declared in the
epistle to Pammachius that "If you shall have loved an alien
woman," that is, the secular knowledge of the heathen, "cut the
woman's hair and cleanse her nails," *et cetera.* So we are in-
structed by the Lateran Council.

I make a further point in considering the question whether it
is expedient to construct a new philosophy or to retain the old.
In ancient times the servant philosophy who became haughty to
her mistress theology was driven out as was Hagar. The sons of
Israel are therefore in part called Jewish and in part Azotic. As
Esdras desired, the alien wives were seized and cast out by the
sons of Judah; that is, by the doctrines of the saints. As we have
shown and Galileo does not cease to show, the sciences will be
restored by examining the world, the book of God. Saint Thomas
says in the *Summa Theologica,* I, question 1, articles 5 ff., that
unbelievers are quoted in theological works as witnesses against
themselves, not as judges or as witnesses against us. It is a
marvel, and one which amazed Bembo, that the unbelieving
heathen not only are received as masters, but as masters of the
theologians. I pause with this.

Because knowledge should be Christian, they lack understanding who forbid and prohibit philosophy among the followers of

Christ. They are similar to the Emperor Julian, [26] who outlawed from the faith and interdicted all the sciences of the Christians. As a result theology, now destitute of her servants, could not call men to the towers of the city of God. This misfortune Saint Thomas discusses in the *Reply,* and calls them Julianites who demanded that monks be forbidden to read secular books and sought to bar us from study of the book of Christ, which is the world. The Scripture of God provides them no excuse. Truly the words, "Be ye unwilling to know more than is proper," and, "Who is seen to be wise for himself is foolish," are not against us. On the contrary, they support us. God does not prohibit philosophic inquiry, but rather inquiry concerning things beyond philosophy, as if we knew all and at our pleasure placed human wisdom above revealed doctrine; or as Gentiles and heretics presumed to circumscribe divine truth and to place the gleaming lamp of Scripture under the Aristotelian bushel. Only because of such presumption does the Book of Job criticize human wisdom, and Isaiah castigate astrologers. It now is established that [within their spheres] wisdom is a divine virtue and astrology a useful science. When Machiavellianism is exalted above divinity, and when man excludes God and considers his proper study an inquiry into what is above nature, human wisdom is properly condemned. Astrology is justly rebuked when, like that ancient astrology which raised itself above the prophets in Babylon, it presumes to predict with certainty events not subject to prophecy, or when by conjecture as to future occurrences, it handicaps a sober analysis of affairs. So I state emphatically regarding the other sciences.

Appendix. It is an essential part of the glory of the Christian religion that we permit [Galileo's] method of discovering new knowledge and of rectifying the old. By so doing we may not be required to cleanse the nails and hair of the heathen. We have begged our philosophy from condemned Gentiles, as if we would make them our superiors. Nevertheless, it is necessary for the glory of our religion that we permit, not the continued insults of Machiavelli and Julian, but that men may observe Christ and the wisdom of God. This point we discussed above, citing Saint

Augustine, and more extensively in *Anti-Machiavelli,* where we say that approbation of science by Christianity may prove a great bond among those other bonds which bind me to the Church of God. This I believe. Why now do we break this bond?

[27]   EXAMINATION OF THE FIFTH ASSERTION

I have shown that liberty of thought is more vigorous in Christian than in other nations. Should this be true, whosoever prescribes at his own pleasure bounds and laws for human thought, as if this action were in harmony with the decrees of Holy Scripture, he not only is irrational and harmful, but also is irreligious and impious. I say as much of him who teaches and accepts no interpretation but his own, and subjects Scripture to his beliefs or to those of a second writer. Such a practice exposes Holy Scripture to the jest of philosophers and the derision of unbelievers and heretics. It closes one avenue to faith and calls men from, rather than to the high tower of devotion. It creates infidels and injures the Holy Spirit. Augustine in *The Christian Doctrine,* Saint Chrysostom writing on the Psalms, Ambrose and Origen in all their works, and Gregory in *Morals,* XV, declare that analysis of the varied meanings of Scripture may be most pregnant and fruitful. Effective discussion is made sterile by bondage. As Augustine teaches in I *Of the Trinity,* Saint Thomas in *Summa Theologica,* I, question 1, article 10, and Cardinal Cajetan, Scripture is most fruitful in meaning when interpreted both in the mystical and in the literal sense. Indeed, as Saint Thomas sets forth in I, question 32, article 4, a passage in Holy Writ may be given all interpretations and expositions which do not di ectly or indirectly contradict other Biblical passages.

In the fashion of many commentators, Saint Thomas presents in his *Tract Against the Errors of the Greeks,* X, question 18, the sound and equitable position which Augustine announced in the first chapter of his *Commentary on Genesis*: "To the end that they may be protected from the distressing ridicule of secular writers, the words of the Scriptures are expounded in many ways." He further declared in *Of the Trinity* that this practice is one among the various methods by which the cavils of heretics are avoided. In the preface to his *Tract,* Saint Thomas states: "I first assert that many Scriptural passages do not pertain to dogmas of faith but rather to doctrines of philosophy. It does great violence to such passages to affirm or to deny them as if they are pertinent to these dogmas. Augustine said truly in *Confession V,* 'When I hear an erroneous opinion set forth by any Christian who is ignorant of what philosophers have determined regarding the heaven and stars, and the motions of Sun and Moon, I look with tolerance upon the man and his opinion. Although he is ignorant of the order and nature of the universe, I do not consider him injured if he believes nothing unworthy of the Lord and Creator of all. He is injured however if he affirms obstinately what he is ignorant of, and considers scientific beliefs a part of the doctrines of faith.'

"That such a conception of scientific opinion is patently prejudicial to our religion, [28] Augustine again states in the initial chapter of his commentary on Genesis: 'It is greatly to be guarded against, and is pernicious and shameful for a Christian to speak of physical phenomena as if he were discussing Scripture. Because of this practice some infidel will declaim foolishly. Regardless of the theory advanced by the Christian, if the phenomena of heaven are observed to depart from the hypothesis, the heathen scarcely will restrain his laughter. Nor is it the great misfortune that human theories should be found incorrect, but that our Christian writers are rebuked as ignorant and are thought to believe erroneous hypotheses by men without the faith, men concerning whose salvation we are troubled because of their utter decay. It therefore appears to me desirable that we understand the spheres of philosophy and of our faith do not conflict, and that theories of philosophy are not to be defended as are the dogmas of faith. New theories always may be introduced under the name of philosophy, and such theories should not be opposed on the grounds that they are contrary to faith, nor should worldly wisdom be given occasion to condemn the doctrines of faith.'" Thus Saint Thomas declares with Augustine. From these statements it is apparent that our contemporaries who support Aristotelianism as a doctrine of faith because Saint Thomas expounded this philosophy, do so ignorantly and in opposition to the Fathers. Indeed, as I shall demonstrate more fully in Chapter IV, Saint Thomas teaches that Aristotelianism is not a doctrine of faith.

Among those who challenge natural philosophy in the name of faith is Ulisse Albergotti, who affirms the Moon shines with her own light because Scripture says, "The Moon shall not give her light." His argument is based upon use of the word *her,* but the passage permits many other interpretations. However, the astonishing thing is that having been correct in their major premise regarding the separate spheres of Scripture and philosophy, Augustine and other Fathers erred in the proposition of their syllogism. Lactantius declared in the *Divine Institutions,* III, 25, and Augustine in XVI *The City of God* that antipodes do not exist, because the men thought to be there could not come from the loins of Adam. Therefore the existence of antipodes contradicts Scripture, which describes all men as created from one. To this argument they add scientific evidence. In the year of our Lord 500, Procopius Gaza built from the writings of all the Fathers a chain of interpretations of Scripture, and proved by them that antipodes do not exist. Because of the Fathers' statements and the authority of Holy Scripture, Saint Ephrem placed the earthly paradise in the opposite hemisphere discovered by Columbus. Indeed, those writers who supposed antipodes were judged heretics by various Fathers. Nevertheless, many navigators have demonstrated the falsity of their opinion. If the existence of antipodes is contrary to the Scripture of God, as these Fathers declared; or if there is an earthly paradise or hell or purgatory, as Dante, Isidore and others have believed, it follows that the truth disclosed by Columbus is discordant with or contrary to Divine Scripture.

In harmony with the philosopher Xenophanes, Procopius and others state that our earth is founded on the waters and floats upon them.[29] They prove this belief from David's lines in Psalm 135, "He founded the earth upon the waters," and Psalm 123, "He established it upon the seas." But the earth now is seen hanging in the middle of the world, sustaining itself and the waters, and not sustained by the seas below. Nor according to nature could the waters be placed underneath the earth unless they were at its center, for in the ordering of nature's system the several parts seek the center, and one and all practice this conservation. The parts of the Sun likewise push toward the center of the Sun and the parts of the Moon to the center of the Moon. What anxiety tormented Saint Ambrose because the movement of heaven could not be explained by rising and falling motion, with the result that with Chrysostom and other Fathers he inclined to belief in its quiescence. But such arguments have little weight in science, and it is wrong and pernicious to set them forth as if matters of faith.

Moreover, Bishop Philastrius described certain beliefs as part of the Christian faith which are contrary to it, and was ridiculed by both Catholic and heretic for his assertions that the age of the world is as great as that which he computed, and that when God breathed into Adam the breath of life, he did not give life to Adam but rather the Holy Spirit. Bede was more cautious when he maintained that dropsy may arise from a fault of the bladder. So was Saint Thomas when he stated under the influence of Aristotle and despite Albertus and Avicenna that men could not live on the equator. Because these opinions were not considered matters of faith (as Saint Thomas regarded that of the flaming sword), they were refuted by evidence from geography and medicine without injury to religion. But the theologians erred abominably who taught the torrid zone of the earth was the flaming sword of the angel guarding the road to paradise, for it has been found that this zone does not impede travellers and navigators. What said the unbelievers and Mohammedans when they heard this notion maintained as a doctrine in harmony with Christian Scripture? We may reply to the censure of the Mohammedans, for they suppose the existence of seven earths under this earth, sustained by cattle and fish, with the head in the east and tail in the west. Yet it is small consolation to publish abroad the faults of others when we err ourselves.

If Galileo shall have demonstrated conclusively the things which he affirms, they shall bring forth among heretics no slight

mockery of our Roman theology. Particularly is this true since
both his hypothesis and the telescope have been accepted with
avidity by many men in Germany, France, England, Poland, Den-
mark, and Sweden. If the hypothesis of Galileo be false, it will
not disturb theological doctrine, [30] for not all that is untrue
is contrary to faith in the militant Church, although peradventure
it may be in the Church triumphant. Indeed, were all that is false
contrary to faith, our discovery of the errors of the Saints in
natural philosophy had proved them heretics. Moreover if Galileo's theory be unsound, it will not endure. I believe therefore
that his type of philosophy should not be forbidden. We are
aware how vigorously the Ultramontanes complained because of
the decrees of the Council of Trent. The new philosophy will be
embraced eagerly by heretics and we shall be ridiculed. What
shall they think when they hear we have rebelled against physics
and astronomy? Will they not immediately cry out that we block
the way, not only of nature, but of Scripture? This knows Cardinal Bellarmine. [Galileo and others should be permitted to set
forth the Copernican hypothesis, and] because Augustine and
Saint Thomas so believed, it should continue to be permitted, as
it now is permitted, to declare heaven is composed of the fifth
essence, according to the method described by Saint Thomas in
his *Tract Against the Errors of the Greeks,* X, article 39, and as
explained by him in the preface.

EXAMINATION OF THE SIXTH ASSERTION

The sixth statement does not require additional proof. Unless
the new philosophy directly or indirectly opposes Holy Scripture
or the decrees of the Church, it clearly is not a falsehood inimical
to Catholic doctrine. As Saint Thomas and Augustine stated in
the passage quoted above in the fourth section of this division,
ecclesiastical approval may be withheld from an hypothesis and
its indiscreet announcement be forbidden within the Church. I
point out in addition that the works of our teachers of theology
obviously are filled with a multitude of errors drawn from heathen
philosophy, as the notion that earth is founded upon the water,
from Xenophanes; that antipodes do not exist and that the Sun

is carried by night to the northern parts of the earth where because of a mountain it is not seen, as Aristotle states in 2 *Metaphysics;* that men cannot live in the torrid zone; that the earthly paradise is in the fortunate islands, or in the Orient with the Chinese, or near the Moon, or others of this nature. Although they have been demonstrated to be false, these notions have not been declared heretical. Error cannot be found in Galileo. He does not repeat opinion, but builds his hypothesis upon careful observations from the book of the world. Nor does he discuss matters of faith, lest he find himself mocked and Holy Scripture with him. I shall further consider this point in the responses which show that without inconvenience to faith, doctrines far more pernicious have been accepted from Aristotle.

[31]   THE THIRD HYPOTHESIS

For the reason that controversy now exists regarding the natural science set forth in Holy Scripture, whosoever wishes to act as judge in this dispute must know these fundamentals. He must know the method of explaining all mystical and literal meanings of Scripture according to the expositions of saintly Fathers and the book of nature, and by all sciences, especially physical and mathematical observations. He must know that Scripture, which is a book of God, does not contradict nature, the sacred book of God. Scripture and nature must be read by clear-seeing men conversant with all sciences, so that both obvious concords and hidden discords can be disclosed. Nor shall Aristotle or another philosopher decide, or any person sit as judge unless conversant with all doctrines of philosophy. As we read from both parts of the book of God we should expound them with proper interpretation, with the spirit of the Fathers and the most pregnant understanding of Holy Church, and with our minds free from every jealousy and passion which clouds and distorts the judgment. We should not be numbered among those judges whom Horace scorns because of evil thinking:

They esteem nothing good except what pleases them;
They believe it shameful to make way for younger men,
And to confess when old the ruin of what they learned as boys.

When Saint Jerome declared in his epistle to Magnus that the holy writers had been trained in the disciplines of all philosophers, he added, "I entreat you to persuade them (those who had reprimanded him because of his predictions), that with the mole they should not condemn the eyes of the goat, or with the toothless envy those who eat with the teeth." It is only from envy that the opponents of Galileo disturb themselves because of the more exalted genius of the modern. Either they begrudge to others knowledge which they are ignorant of or despair to know, or now that they are called masters, are ashamed again to become disciples.

CONCLUSION OF THE THIRD CHAPTER

It has been proved, as Bernard said, that he who has zeal without knowledge or knowledge without zeal cannot judge of these questions. Nor can he know what things must be known, and that this requirement of knowledge and zeal for God is not desired in behalf of man but in behalf of God. [32] We have before our eyes the passage in Numbers 11 where Joshua, over-zealous because of his loyalty to Moses and unwilling to permit others in the camp to prophesy, heard his leader rebuke him and say: "O that all the people might prophesy, and that the Lord would give them his spirit!" Were he here today Saint Thomas would speak of himself more strongly than did Moses. I am ashamed that men burn with zeal for Aristotle rather than for Saint Thomas or Moses, and that because of unbelievers we forbid Christians to philosophize.

CHAPTER IV

REPLY TO THE ARGUMENTS ADVANCED AGAINST GALILEO
RESPONSE TO THE FIRST

We have answered the first argument against Galileo in the preceding chapter, where we discussed the question of whether it is permissible to accept the new philosophy and by so doing to deprive Aristotelianism of authority. We now say briefly it is heresy to maintain that theology is founded upon Aristotle or stands in need of his approbation of philosophic doctrine. In the second hypothesis I proved from Saint Thomas, *Summa Theologica,* I, question 1, articles 5 ff.; *Tract Against the Errors of the Greeks,* X; and the *Reply,* I, that Aristotle was not considered as a judge in theology or witness against Christians, but as a witness against both his group of unbelievers and other sophisters; and, that what Aristotle says concerning the world, but not what he conjectures regarding it, was presented as representative of the opinions of this group. When Saint Thomas so neglected his own precept as to set forth Aristotle in a theological exposition, he was rebuked in the Articles of Paris. However, he can be excused without impropriety, as I have excused him in the preceding question.

Who condemns Galileo because he contradicts Aristotle, first condemns Augustine, Ambrose, Basil, Eusebius, Origen, Chrysostom, Justin, and other holy teachers of the Church. It is apparent from their works that they not only opposed Aristotle in metaphysics, but in virtually all physical conceptions, and regarded Plato and the Stoics with greater favor. Indeed Saint Justin, named philosopher and martyr, composed a book with the title *Against Aristotle.* In the fifth section of the second hypothesis of Chapter IV, I demonstrated that they are ignorant and err impiously [33] who believe the destruction of Aristotle will adversely affect theology. I now shall prove the contrary to their belief; unless Aristotle's authority is overthrown, his heresies will destroy us, namely:

THE DEFENSE OF GALILEO 41

(1) Motion is eternal, and if not there is no God. Aristotle affirms this doctrine in VIII, *Physics,* and XII, *Metaphysics.* Saint Thomas also interprets these passages in this fashion in his *De Coelo,* X, and confronts Aristotle with the testimony of Justin and other Fathers.

(2) The soul is immortal, or virtually immortal, in all men.

(3) God has no regard for the lower beings, including mankind, of the world.

(4) God labors against the angels in rotating the spheres.

(5) There is neither reward nor punishment after death.

(6) The infernal region is a fable.

(7) God acts from necessity.

(8) Chance nullifies the design of Providence. With these heresies are many others by which Aristotle challenges the Christian faith. This conclusion also is stated by Saint Thomas, Averroes, Alexander, and various Greeks and Rabbis.

Because of such heresies Saint Vincent, and Master Serafinus de Firmo in his exposition of the apocalypse, call Aristotle the vessel of God's wrath which the third angel poured upon the waters of wisdom. In his book against Celsus, Origen describes him as more evil and impious than Epicurus. Augustine, Ambrose, and Justin, who explain Aristotle according to his true meaning, condemn him vigorously and at length. It is amazing that smatterers in learning should believe theology is founded upon Aristotle, a notion which some of our ecclesiastical brothers fasten upon Saint Thomas. Because of their false interpretation they praise Saint Thomas, just as the equally mistaken theologians of Paris reprimanded him. But Saint Thomas believed quite differently from these commentators, and by creating an antidote from venom, expounded Aristotle for the benefit of the Catholic faith.

Galileo is loyal to the essentials of religion, and prudently describes natural phenomena according to evidence obtained from observation. He does not describe phenomena as conjecture may dictate, or, to follow Aristotle, as he may create from his own mind. Moreover, a refutation of the doctrines of infidels and of the falsehoods of unbelievers strengthens Christianity and does not destroy theology. As we have said before, this truth is one among those which the judge should know. We shall demonstrate elsewhere from the testimony of Nicephorus and other ecclesiastical historians what heresies have developed from Aristotelianism, and show that Aristotle's Averroism was the cradle of Machiavellism. Yet the new philosophy proceeds from the world, the book of God. It humbly serves theology and calls forth witnesses which are neither the fancies of Aristotle nor the dreams of another philosopher.

[34] Response to the Second Argument Against Galileo

In reply to the second argument, I deny that the doctrines of Galileo oppose the beliefs of all Fathers and scholastics. If some of his doctrines are not literally consonant with theirs in meaning, they are consonant in purpose. The Fathers and scholastics desired that truth be presented, and invited not only the testimony of principles of philosophy but also the interpretations which theorists and commentators had set forth. It therefore is proper to evaluate their opinions of the heavens, and to do this by evidence similar in kind to that by which Columbus and Magellan evaluated [placed before] the opinions concerning the earth held by Lactantius, Ephrem, Saint Thomas, Anthony, and other Holy Fathers. In the present response I also show, first, that some theologians have embraced doctrines of philosophy more opposed to the holy teachers and to Scripture than are the theories of Galileo; secondly, that many Fathers and scholastics agree with these theories; and thirdly, that Scripture is more favorable to the doctrine of Galileo than it is to that of his adversaries.

Proof of the First Point. All philosophers teach that heaven is not the fifth essence, but is composed either of elements or (and particularly the stars) of fire alone. This interpretation is advanced by holy Augustine, Ambrose, Basil, Cyril, Chrysostom, Theodoret, Bernard (in his discourse on women and the Sun), and by the Master of the *Sentences* [Peter Lombard]. In the Hexaemeron, IV, Ambrose proves heaven is not an immutable fifth essence from the passage in Scripture, "The heavens will pass away, and grow old as vestments." When he expounds for Christians Aristotle's *De Caelo* against Aristotle, Philoponus makes the same point. Many scholastics declare heaven may be regarded as composed of the fifth essence, and no violence done to Scripture, but Ambrose, together with Justin and Basil, repeatedly execrates this belief as a fiction and a diabolical invention. In the first book of his exposition of Aristotle, Saint Thomas places on one side Moses' description of the Work of the Six Days, and on the other the interpretations of the Fathers and philosophers, and the beliefs of Aristotle. He harmonizes much of the Scriptural text with Aristotle, but teaches in questions 65-67 and 70-71 that Aristotelianism should be opposed. The sciolists have not observed this fact.

Divine Scripture declares the Sun actually is hot and lucid. Genesis employs the words, "greater light." His heat is described in Psalm 18 [19], Ecclesiastes 43, and in many other passages. Wisdom 17 speaks of the power of fire, and of "the bright flames of the stars." Basil, and Ambrose in Hexaemeron, IV, assert that Sun and stars are fire, and that belief to the contrary is heresy. [35] The same conviction is stated by Augustine, Chrysostom, Justin, Bernard, Origen, Philoponus, and all Fathers whose works have been read. The Church sings in the Ambrosian hymn, "Now the fiery Sun departs." Aristotle does not place light in the Sun, and declares in *2 De Caelo,* 42 [7], that light and heat are produced by the friction of air. Simplicius and Alexander state that Aristotle so believed, and Averroes, in his work on the substance of the celestial orbs, describes Aristotle as having removed light and heat from the Sun. According to his belief, the Sun cannot be composed of fire. Our more recent philosophers do not agree with Aristotle, and have returned light to the Sun.

However, all scholastics are permitted to believe the Sun actually is not hot. They suffer from no taint of heresy, nor does the Church censure this opinion. In addition, many modern philosophers contradict in various ways either Aristotle or the literal word of Scripture without incurring proscription of their beliefs. Galileo demonstrates the truth of his doctrines by sensory observation, and is forbidden to read in the book of God! I pass without comment the several conceptions once commonly regarded as matters of faith which the experience of mankind has shown to be false. Among these were the beliefs that antipodes do not exist, and that paradise or hell is located in the opposite hemisphere or in the fortunate islands. Neither shall I mention that by means of the authority of the word of Scripture, Procopius, Eusebius, and others founded earth upon the waters. Those men who demonstrated this notion untrue and now are supported by common knowledge were not condemned by the Church. All these things fight for Galileo.

Proof of the Second Point. Whether the earth stands in the center or beyond the center of the world is not a question which in any way pertains to the dogmas of faith. So declared Saint Thomas in the fourth assertion. This conclusion also was affirmed strongly by the Fathers and scholastics. Among others who concluded that earth is not in the center of the world and that heaven is not round, I mention especially Lactantius, *Divine Institutions,* III, 23, Procopius, Bishop Eusebius, Diodorus, Bishop of Tarsus, and Justin in his *Answers to the Orthodox.* Chrysostom stated the same belief in his sixth and thirteenth homilies on Genesis. He declared in the third homily on the Epistle to the Romans that men are ignorant of the location of hell, a belief also set forth by Augustine, *The City of God,* XXII, 16, by Magister [Peter Lombard], *Sentences,* IV, distinction 44, and by Saint Thomas, *Tract Against the Errors of the Greeks,* XI, 15. Because the Apostle said in Ephesians 4, "Christ descended into the lower parts of the earth," it is believed hell must be located either at the center or within that place in our earth known by the word *lower.* Unless we assume the existence of other and lower earths, hell therefore must be in this part of ours. David implies that Christ travelled to hell, for the Apostle Peter, Acts 2, quotes him as saying to Christ, "Thou wilt not leave my soul in hell." But these statements fail to inform us whether or not earth is in the center of the world. [36] Furthermore, if Christ placed beyond our world the gloomy lower regions which he called *outer darkness,* as Origen surmises in his commentary on Matthew, and Chrysostom in his discourse on Romans, it follows that there may be other universes beyond our world. Because they have read carefully neither Scripture nor the books of the holy Fathers, the censors of Galileo condemn this belief. But passing over controversial questions, we may say with Chrysostom in his seventh homily on I Thessalonians, that this much is known concerning the earth: it is cold, solid, and black. Beyond this we know nothing, especially its place and situation in the universe.

Scripture does not teach us that the earth is in the center more than it teaches the earth is on the circumference of the world. Chrysostom further declares that we do not know whether the earth stands or is moved. As I have said, he concludes that nothing can be ascertained beyond the three mentioned conditions of the earth: its coldness, dryness [solidity?], and blackness. In agreement with Chrysostom are Theophylact and such others as Lactantius, Augustine, Procopius, Diodorus, and Eusebius. Justin contends the earth is not in the center of the world. I cannot understand why our present theologians, lacking both Divine Revelation and the demonstrations or experiments of scientists, judge themselves to know beyond all question that earth stands immobile in the center of the universe. Nor can I conceive how they may regard the contrasting hypothesis as opposed to Fathers and scholastics whose works they have not read.

If it be true, as is believed by Gregory and other Fathers, that hell is in the center and has within it a fire which tortures the damned, it is necessary that the earth should move. Aristotle testifies that Pythagoras, who located the place of punishment in the center of the earth and made fire the cause of motion, described earth as mobile and animate. So Ovid believes in 15 *Metamorphoses,* Origen in his commentary on Ezechiel, Alexander Aphrodisaeus, and Plato. For the reason that the existence of hell in the center of the earth is contrary to nature and yet cannot be regarded as a miracle, Saint Thomas in the *Tract,* XI, 24, assigns it to another and unknown place. It is essential, if hell be in the center of the earth, for earth to be hot within, and, according to Gregory and others cited in the argument of Saint Thomas, to be mobile. The interpretation of Galileo does not oppose the belief of Saint Gregory, but rather that of Aristotle.

That the starry heaven is immobile is taught by Procopius, Diodorus, Eusebius, and Justin. In numerous places Chrysostom proves by reason and Scripture that heaven does not move, [including] his commentary on I Thessalonians, homily 12 to the people of Antioch, and homilies 14 and 27 on Hebrews. The Apostle Paul said in Hebrews 8 that heaven is the tabernacle of the priest Christ, "Which the Lord hath pitched, and not man," and declares heaven is fixed, not mobile. [37] Similarly in chapter 12 and particularly in chapter 10 of his commentary on Genesis, II, Augustine narrates that by unquestionable demonstrations, the mathematicians of his day proved heaven immobile. Truly, we should not repudiate the judgment of philosophers in physical things without careful and sufficient consideration. Neither should we put theology and ourselves to scorn by so doing. Furthermore, the Fathers did not regard heaven as round or mobile, for such a belief is opposed by Moses, the Prophets, and by Psalm 103 [104], which says in the words of Chrysostom, "Who reareth the heaven as a vault, and stretchest it out as a pavilion." Justin observes that there had been controversy between Christians and unbelievers because the Christians held with Scripture that heaven is immobile.

Copernicus demonstrates by logic that since heaven surrounds all things, it is immobile. We believe with Basil that heaven is composed of vital heat greatly extended. Bede, Strabo, and the Fathers I have mentioned, say the starry Firmament is that which Moses called the Firmament, and because it is called *Firmament,* they regard it as firm and stable. David wrote that "The word of the Lord makes firm the heaven," and Paul declared, "God fixed it." If the moderns deny with Scripture that heaven is immobile, this hypothesis will not be heresy.

Because the Fathers themselves regarded heaven as fixed and non-spherical, it is amazing that the opponents of Galileo should declare his doctrine contrary to theirs. My interpretation that the Fathers commonly considered heaven neither round nor mobile is supported by the similar interpretation presented by Sixtus Senensis in the *Bibliotheca Sancta*. Peter Lombard, Master of all scholastics, and well-versed in the doctrines of the Fathers, said in *Sentences* II, distinction 14, "The Holy Spirit does not declare what figure heaven may be." He then inquired whether heaven is mobile or immobile, and whether this question may be answered with certainty from Holy Scripture. The Master noted, for example, that heaven is called the Firmament, and that not heaven but the stars in it are moved, for the stars are not placed there as knots in a board. Having observed the motion of the stars and the structure of heaven, which makes firm what is firm, he was able to satisfy himself regarding celestial appearances. He therefore inclines toward the belief of Galileo. Despite the assertions made by the enemies of the Florentine, neither the Fathers nor the scholastics definitely concluded that earth stands and heaven is moved.

Proof of the Third Point. In his commentary on *De Caelo,* II, chapter 20 and following, Saint Thomas examines the opinion of Aristotle regarding the motion of the earth and stability of heaven. He does not state, as he always is accustomed to state in discussing the doctrines of Aristotle and other philosophers, that the hypothesis of the rotation of the earth is opposed to Holy Scripture. In the *Tract,* X, 16, where he questions whether the motion of the earth may contradict Scripture, he specifically declares that its axial rotation is contrary to Aristotle, not contrary to Scripture. (He is here discussing the questions of whether earth can be turned on its axis or be moved by angels.) If the arrangement of a universe created and ordered by God is declared unalterable because of some human theory regarding the position and immobility of its parts, [38] this theory, Saint Thomas rightly observes, is itself contrary to Scripture. Whatsoever modern theologians may say, it follows inevitably, first, either the Firmament stands, or it is not against the Christian faith to affirm that it stands; and secondly, either the earth is moved, or it is not contrary to Christian faith to affirm its motion.

I have said that many Fathers regard heaven as fixed, among

whom are the Master of the *Sentences,* Chrysostom, Lactantius, Procopius, and Augustine. Sixtus Senensis rightly states that the belief in a mobile heaven held by the vulgar is contrary to Scripture. Since those who maintain that heaven moves are unable to discern the manner in which the stars appear to be moved, and whether they are placed in the Firmament as the Master says (who does not fix them there as knots in a board), they are forced to declare that the unmoved Firmament which we see is a starless space beyond heaven. However, Moses places stars in the Firmament, and both the holy Bede and Strabo assert the Firmament is the starry heaven. It appears that these men, whom Saint Thomas praises, and who follow accurately the meaning of Scripture, necessarily regard the Firmament as the place where the stars are located. Saint Thomas notes however that it is irrational for the Fathers to state in explanation of celestial phenomena that the stars (but not the Firmament), appear to be or may be moved in precisely the same fashion as the planets. There are innumerable stars in the Firmament, especially in the galaxy, and [apparently?] they always preserve in their constellations the same relative situation, order, and motion. But it scarcely is possible for perpetual order to be preserved in so great a multitude of stars. In fact, since some are more remote from the earth and others nearer, some change in relative place should at the least have produced a varying arrangement of local position. Because some stars are large, others small, and their virtue unequal, they can no more be moved with one and the same motion than can the several different planets. They require a variety of motions in keeping with the planets, which are moved differently because they vary in magnitude or virtue, whether they are turned by themselves or by the Sun.

Simplicius employs such an argument to prove that heaven is not composed of fire, and declares the stars are moved as fishes move in the sea, with many variations and inequalities, and do not remain continually in the same position. But our argument is stronger than that of Simplicius. If the Fathers are correct when they say the Firmament stands unmoved, the stars stand with it. When the Master of the *Sentences* [Peter Lombard], Saint

Chrysostom, and other Fathers declare in harmony with Catholic faith that the Firmament is unmoved, it is necessary that they state the same of the stars much more vigorously. [Since the stars are immobile] it follows that the earth is carried about as a ship, and that the stars appear to be moved just as from a ship an island or a tower on the shore seems in motion. [39] The hypothesis of the rotation of the earth unquestionably is sound, and without absurdity or distortion satisfies Scriptural statements concerning the unmoved Firmament, where God placed the stars. Because he was accustomed to revere the Fathers, Saint Thomas was aware of and touched upon this point, and so testifies of himself in his *Tract,* I. The Fathers and the two masters of the scholastics, Saint Thomas and Peter Lombard, support more than they oppose Galileo, and Scripture favors more than it censures him.

RESPONSE TO THE THIRD ARGUMENT AGAINST GALILEO

I reply to the third argument that the passage in Psalm 92 [93], "He hath established the earth, which shall not be moved," refers only to a local position and order which preserves itself firm and continually and wholly unchanged. The similar statement, "He hath founded the earth upon its own bases: it shall not be moved for ever and ever," describes only the time when heaven was moved and the earth bounded. So the Church sings with the Prophet, and the adversaries of Galileo grant that this interpretation is reasonable. Those who maintain that the Firmament rather than the earth is moved may be answered with the argument that Scripture employed the word *Firmament* because what is described maintains an unvaried stability with reference to both arrangement and motion. We read in Job that the solid heavens are spread out as if they are air. Basil teaches from Scriptural authority that they are composed of the most subtle air, and expounds in various ways their firmness. Proverbs 8 says in behalf of Galileo, "When he prepared the heavens I was present: when with a certain law and compass he enclosed the abyss. When he established the sky above, and poised the fountains of waters." In this passage we find the aethereal heaven made firm by God, the fountains poured out, *et cetera*. Further-more, David wrote that the heavens were made firm by the word of the Lord. Holy Scripture says no more of the firmness of the earth than it says of the firmness of heaven. For the reason that those who move the heavens do not contradict the Scripture of God, neither do those who move the earth. Scripture permits both interpretations. In their explanation of Psalm 135 [136], "Who established the earth above the waters," the impugners of Galileo reject the words *above the waters*. For a similar reason, Galileo rejects *established*. This he contends was apparently spoken in the same way as *above the waters* [that is, figuratively]. The second passage, which states that earth abideth forever, undoubtedly contrasts the condition of enduring with that of passing away. For some are dead, others are born, says Solomon, but the earth stands or remains in its usual condition, nor will it ever perish in complete disintegration.

I also add that if the reasons advanced by Saint Thomas are sound, and if hell is in the center of the earth (as many of the learned and all of the vulgar believe), it almost is essential to the Christian faith that the fire-heated earth be mobile and be-yond the center of the world. It is the nature of fire and of an animate thing to move. [40] In the *Tract*, XI, 24, Saint Thomas does not declare hell is in the center of the earth, for he believes the earth is cold, that all heavy things move to its center, and, [were hell there] the universe could not be kept within its bounds. Nor could a miracle be performed, because hell is the result of natural processes ("For Tophet is prepared from yesterday," says Isaiah 30). Augustine wrote truly that within these processes there is only nature and no miracle. According to Saint Thomas it therefore is necessary either that earth is hot, mobile, and on the periphery [of the world], or that hell is not located in its center.

RESPONSE TO THE FOURTH ARGUMENT

I reply to the fourth argument against Galileo that in the statements and text of Solomon the word *standeth* obviously does not describe earth as immobile, but as free from degeneration or disintegration. Solomon says, "One generation passeth away and another generation cometh, but the earth standeth forever," that is, man dies, but the earth does not. Indeed, Job says of the corruptibility of man, "He never remains in the same state." The passage from Solomon which speaks of the rising and returning of the Sun, and of his revolving about the north, may also be variously interpreted without rejection of Scripture. Augustine, Lactantius, and others understand from it that the Sun does not revolve around the earth, but moves about its northern side, and because of an intervening mountain of great size is not seen by us. Aristotle relates in 2 *Meteorum* that Xenophanes and other ancient philosophers advanced this conception when they denied the existence of antipodes. Because the conception would not permit antipodes, Augustine approved it. In harmony with the thinking of Ptolemy, Saint Thomas expresses in his *Tract, X, 28,* and XI, 6, the belief that the Sun is moved by angelic spirits. Nevertheless, he declares in the latter passage that to the end Scripture may better avoid the derision of philosophers, Solomon's statement and other Biblical texts have many interpretations. I therefore am permitted to expound his statement in another fashion, and avoid the ridicule of the Germans who now have demonstrated that earth is moved and the Sun stands in the center, among them Copernicus, Reinhold, Stadius, Maestlin, and Kepler. This theory also is maintained by Gilbert and innumerable English and French; and by the Italians Francesco Maria of Ferrara, Giovanni Antonio Magini, Cardinal Cusanus, Colantonus Stelliola and others. As I mentioned in the second hypothesis of the third chapter, it was supported in antiquity by Pythagoras and all his followers, and by Heraclitus [Heraclides of Pontus?], Aristarchus, Philolaus and others. I pointed out in the response to the second argument against Galileo that Saint Thomas does not condemn as heretical the hypothesis advanced by the Pythagoreans.

However, if Saint Thomas had condemned this hypothesis, it would not suddenly have become heresy. [41] Saint Chrysostom declared it heresy against Scripture and the Church to affirm the existence of many spheres and heavens [, but the followers of Aristotle have not been condemned]. Philastrius makes those heretics who do not accept his notion regarding the age of the world. Ambrose asserts it is heresy to say the Sun is not actually hot, and some modern theologians call the philosopher a heretic who demonstrates that the Moon shines with borrowed light. Procopius so describes him who denies earth is founded on the waters. The scholastics hold contrary beliefs in all these things, but they are not heretics. Scripture allows many interpretations, and the Church has not passed judgment. Therefore permit Galileo to interpret Solomon's text in a different manner; namely: the Sun moves according to sense and appearances. Saint Thomas states in the *Summa Theologica,* I, question 70, articles 1-3, that Moses so speaks as to accommodate sensible things to the popular and not to the philosophic belief. In the response to 5, *ibidem,* he replies with Chrysostom that although many stars are larger than the Moon, Moses calls the Moon a great light because of its effect upon us and according to our senses.

In our day astronomers have placed four moons around Jupiter. There also are two which revolve about Saturn, just as Mercury and Venus revolve about the Sun. If Moses did not accommodate his speech to human sense, and if men actually inhabit Jupiter, he would have said, "God made five great lights, the Sun the greater light, and the Medicean planets four smaller lights." The Medicean planets appear as great to the senses of the inhabitants of Jupiter as the Moon appears to the senses of us who live on the earth. As we demonstrate in the second hypothesis from the sayings of Chrysostom, Augustine, Thomas, Origen, Bede, and all the Fathers, the entire Scripture accommodates its discourse in syntax and meaning to the external senses of the common people. Indeed, God left the world, his first Scripture, to the disputes of men, and within the limits prescribed by the Church, Divine Wisdom also left to their disputes variant meanings of his second Scripture. So Christ, the incarnate wisdom of God (as Origen taught), man himself among the ignorant and the young, prophet among teachers, displayed God to spiritual men. The world is wisdom in material form, and shows us more as we have more capacity. To this end Divine Wisdom wrote Scripture.

RESPONSE TO THE FIFTH AND SIXTH ARGUMENTS

In response to the fifth and sixth arguments I deny that the two miracles of Joshua and Hezekiah are destroyed by placing the mansion of the Sun in the center of the world. The Sun is said to have stood and to have been turned back in harmony with sensory observation, when in fact the earth ceased to move [42] and was turned back by a true miracle. It is not a greater miracle for the Sun to have stood than for the earth to have suspended rotation. When the Church sings in the hymn, "Now the fiery Sun departs," you may without heresy interpret the word *fiery* equivocally, and as descriptive of the Sun's appearance to us rather than of its true nature. In like manner I gloss *departs* in the hymn and *turned back* in Isaiah as having a double meaning —for us, although not for the Sun. Virgil said [speaking as from the ship], "We are carried forward, and the lands and cities recede"; when on the contrary we recede and not the cities.

My gloss of the word *departs* is less dissonant with the text of the hymn than is that which interprets the word *fiery* as figurative. It is stated in the final volume of the works of Saint Ambrose that he wrote the hymn. In the *Hexaemeron,* Saint Ambrose both proves and expresses his personal belief that the Sun is composed of actual fire, and declares contrary ideas are heresy or fatuity. In keeping with the Fathers cited in the second response, he also flays vigorously the Aristotelians. The Church now sings this hymn, has made it his symbol of Athanasius, and the hymn itself overflows with many interpretations that are abundant in meaning. However, these things do not make heretics of those who deny [Ambrose's belief] that the Sun actually is hot, unless they condemn it affirmatively. But those who declare there is no miracle recorded in Joshua and Hezekiah [Isaiah] unless the accounts are interpreted according to the error of sensory perception, condemn affirmatively and oppose Scripture. We say however that the miracle is the same if the earth suspends rotation, for as perspective teaches, the optical effect is identical in observing actual motion and that which is only apparent. Miracles are miracles to us, not to God, whom nothing amazes. They were created because of us, not because of God, and, as the

Apostle says, because unbelievers are so many. It is nevertheless clear that when God gave his command [through Joshua], the Sun ceased to move in the same fashion that it had moved; that is, it ceased to move according to appearances.

It is in the popular manner that God is said to have made the Moon a great light. He who declares with Chrysostom that the Moon is great only in respect to us neither conceals a truth nor opposes the divine [creative] action. Nor is Chrysostom lower than Epicurus and Lucretius, who consider the stars exactly as large as they appear to be. When we call the Moon truly a great light, do we not accept the interpretation of the unscientific, impious Epicurus, and reject the conclusion Chrysostom developed by mathematics, in order to uphold the belief of the vulgar? Human observation has determined that the rainbow of heaven is made on a mist which intercepts and changes the rays of the Sun, as is well known in physics. But the Scripture of God says in Genesis 9 that so often as it rains, God will place this sign in the clouds in memory of himself and [as a token of] our security, because no more will he cover the earth with inundating waters. If anyone rejects either this text or the findings of natural philosophy, and believes the rainbow should be attributed neither to God nor to the Sun, he lacks both intelligence and knowledge of the Scriptures. [43] Whatsoever nature creates is the work of God. Indeed, nature is divine law and precept, as is proved by Chrysostom, and by Ambrose in the *Hexaemeron*. When God says in Joshua that the Sun stands and is not moved, whosoever declares this miracle is lessened by belief in rotation of the earth, does not exalt miracle. On the contrary, and in the fashion of the philosopher who does not praise the rainbow of God, he states only in what manner it was made, of what material, and by what cause and design.

RESPONSE TO THE SEVENTH ARGUMENT AGAINST GALILEO

The seventh argument is easily answered. Deborah and Juda describe the wandering and the courses of the planets rather than the movements of the stars. Nor are the stars placed in heaven as knots in a board, as Aristotle believed, but are moved individually and by themselves. So the Master of the *Sentences* and all Fathers declare with Augustine. Because of the authority of Chrysostom's interpretation, Saint Thomas was moved to agree in the *Summa Theologica,* I, question 70, article 1, more with Ptolemy than with Aristotle, and says with all the Pythagoreans that the stars are not fixed as knots in a board. He also teaches here that the part of heaven in which the planets are thought to be moved is the lower and not the higher portion of the Firmament.

We concede to Esdras that the Sun turned about the heavens. But Esdras does not say the Sun is moved; rather that he wheeled and turned the spheres with their planets. This may be understood to mean that by his light the Sun moved the planets about, an hypothesis which Pliny also supports in his *Natural History,* II. It is however more probable that the Sun does not move the spheres, but instead moves the air and vapor which make a vaporous orbit around the planets, as Galileo and the Pythagoreans show and as Copernicus implies when he speaks of the great orbit of the earth. Although Chrysostom desired that the stars be fixed, he declared it sufficient if they were turned about, since in this way it could be said that the heaven which contains them revolves. The mathematicians of the time of Augustine who, as he himself says, proved the immobility of heaven by infallible demonstrations, could not have proved this of the planets, but only of the heaven and of the stars therein. But as Copernicus, Galileo, and the Pythagoreans pointed out, heaven cannot be proved stable by any mathematical method except that of calculating the relationship of the earth and the fixed stars and planets. Augustine's use of the word *infallible* indicates adequately that he regarded heaven as immobile, although the calculations were perhaps inadequate. Nevertheless, as I state in the second hypothesis and in the response to it, Augustine advised us that we not assert the contrary as if it were a matter of faith. See the *Commentary* of Augustine, II, on Genesis 10. [44]

It is sufficient that the swift movement of the Sun described in Esdras is interpreted as the movement of axial rotation, which Telesio proved by rational deduction, and Galileo by the motion of the spots rotating with the Sun. The Sun therefore is turned about itself and not about the earth. You will say, as you have said before, that this explanation appears adequate.

RESPONSE TO THE EIGHTH ARGUMENT

I answer to this argument that it apparently is not so much against Scripture to place waters in heaven as the opposite belief is contrary both to Scripture and the Catholic faith. If, as Scripture states, there are waters above heaven, it is necessary that lands be there. The waters cannot be retained except by the solidity of earth. Certainly they cannot be supported by the thinness of the most subtle heaven or by the heat of the stars. The latter would dissolve them into mist. Because some theologians fear this consequence, they maintain the waters are frozen.

Moses said of old in Genesis 1 that the Firmament divided the waters that are under the Firmament from those that are above the Firmament. David wrote in Psalm 103 [104], "Who stretchest out the heaven like a pavilion; who coverest the higher rooms thereof with water," and in 148, "Let all the waters that are above the heavens praise the name of the Lord." Daniel repeats this in the song, and so does all Scripture. Origen understood the waters above the heavens to be angels of a watery nature, but was opposed by Saint Basil. Having explained the waters after the fashion of Origen in his *Confessions,* XIII, 18, Saint Augustine recanted later in Book II, retraction 6.

In the *Summa Theologica,* I, question 68, article 1, Saint Thomas discusses the threefold interpretation of the substance of the Firmament. The first is that of Empedocles and various Pythagoreans, who compounded the Firmament of the four elements, and by this interpretation explain simply and without difficulty the meaning found in the two statements by Moses: that actual waters exist in heaven and in the stars, and that the Firmament was created on the second day. Heaven is said to have been made in the beginning, and the Firmament created the second day is called heaven by God. The second of the three interpretations is that of Plato, who constructs the Firmament of a substance with the nature of fire. I find nevertheless in *Timaeus* the belief and reasoning of Plato that there may be four elements, and Ficino himself permits symbols of [three] elements to be understood there: the solidity of earth, the transpicuity of water, and the motion of air, together with fire that is virtually actual in light and heat. Saint Thomas acknowledges however that he had not read Plato, for at that time Plato in Latin was not yet revered.

The text of Moses, declares Saint Thomas, conflicts in two particulars with the interpretation that the Firmament is of the nature of fire. [45] First, if the Firmament was constructed following the thought of Plato, it was made when the element of fire was created. Now production of the elements [including fire], was the work [of the first stage] of the creation, as is understood by all from the passage, "In the beginning God created heaven and earth." According to all the Fathers, Moses's account of the Six Days refers only to the adornment of heaven and earth. Discrepancy therefore results, for the Firmament was made the second day, and is the work of adornment rather than of initial creation. Whatever is urged in behalf of Plato's belief will be frivolous, for his interpretation causes the element fire to be created after the element of fire has been created. Secondly, there is discord because the fiery Firmament of Plato does not permit the waters above the heavens truthfully to be described as actual waters. In what manner can such a Firmament be joined with the waters?

Because they believed heaven is fiery in nature, Basil and Chrysostom replied to both these objections. Chrysostom responded to the initial criticism, that Moses first stated that in the beginning, "God made heaven and earth," and subsequently described all things of the creation separately, according to the manner in which they were made. Basil answered differently, and said that the statements of Moses descriptive of the first day refer to the immobile empyreal heaven, and those of the day following to the heaven of the stars. He replied to the second objection that the waters above the Firmament exist to temper the heat of the empyreum; they are ice and therefore do not run down. He asserted that by the word Firmament, solid air may be understood, and that the waters which produce rain are made above it, so that Scripture said, "The waters above the Firmament" *et cetera*. Nevertheless, Basil himself contended, and Ambrose and Magister [Peter Lombard], that the waters are true waters. Saint Bonaventure believed the same, and Bede, and most of the Fathers, who thought also that the starry heaven was made of the waters, with the frozen waters placed above it. Augustine conceded in his *Commentary on Genesis,* II, 3, that the stars are made of fire and the starry heaven is fire, but later was drawn to the opinion that little by little the waters were raised above heaven, as solid vapor is raised above the air, and now may be called the Firmament. The Master of the *Sentences* quotes this opinion without condemning it. In their various explanations the Fathers and scholastics torture in different ways the text of Moses by absurdities which naturally follow if the starry heaven is considered mobile and not as composed of the four elements.

The final part of the threefold interpretation is the opinion of Aristotle adduced by Saint Thomas: that the starry heaven is an unchangeable fifth essence. However, Saint Thomas confesses regarding this interpretation that by it he is much less able to explain satisfactorily the meaning of Scripture. The Firmament now is said to have been made on the second day from pre-existing material created on the first day. More probably, according to Saint Thomas, this substance was created prior to all the days, for Moses says, "In the beginning God created heaven and earth. And the earth was [46] void and empty, and the Spirit of God moved over the waters." For the reason that it could not be explained to unlearned people except in terms of corporeal forms, Augustine understands that material substance was meant by the words earth and waters, as Saint Thomas also says in the *Summa Theologica,* I, question 68, article 1. In the argument presented by Saint Thomas, which follows that of Aristotle, heaven is by its own nature incorruptible, and therefore contains substance which could not exist in other forms.

Under the interpretation of Aristotle it is impossible that the Firmament was made the second day. We therefore cannot say that Moses placed actual waters above the Firmament, although Sacred Scripture and the Fathers teach that he did. Nor do the

Fathers speak truthfully when they declare the waters from below ascend bit by bit above the Firmament. Some theologians assert in support of Aristotle that the waters above the Firmament are the empyreal heaven, and that Scripture describes this as aqueous because it possesses a diaphaneity similar to water. For such a reason still others call the Firmament crystalline, and also make it immobile. Because Saint Thomas saw that the interpretation of Aristotle could be defended only with difficulty, he defends it all, and answers in its support that the Firmament divides the waters from the waters; that is, it divides the primary material (by which name Augustine describes the waters), if the Firmament is composed of the fifth essence.

But all of these beliefs, established to harmonize interpretations of Plato with Moses, and of Aristotle with Moses, are filled with labyrinthian difficulties, and twist the text of Scripture to the mystical sense. In truth, they reduce it to absurdity. Augustine teaches in *The Christian Doctrine* that where the literal meaning of Scripture may be ascertained, we should not fly to the mystical, [nor set it forth] unless first the literal meaning is presupposed and declared. In the *Commentary on Genesis,* II, he praises the conclusion of Basil that the Firmament is composed of air, because this interpretation is not opposed to faith and once proof has been presented, can be promptly accepted. For the reason that it did not adversely affect his doctrine of a heaven composed entirely of fire, Telesio approved the conception. We value Basil's conclusion above all others, and know of none better.

If the observations of Galileo are trustworthy, I see further difficulties in accepting a majority of the interpretations discussed. The first of these questionable interpretations is the opinion of Chrysostom that Moses recapitulates on the second day what had been made during a period prior to the days of creation. This opinion does not appear credible, and many of the Fathers oppose it. Indeed, as Augustine, Thomas, and Magister teach, all the Fathers suppose [not the making but rather] preparation during the period before the day of creation. I reply to Basil's belief that the immobile empyrean was created the first day and the starry heaven the second, that this belief does not satisfy all requirements, and was developed without the testimony of Scripture for the purpose of supporting strongly an interpretation. [47]

Using the statements of Porphyrius, Augustine in *The City of God*, X, describes the empyreal heaven as identical with the starry heaven, and says it is called empyrean; that is, fire. The stars are composed of fire, for Wisdom 18 speaks of the "bright flames of the stars." Heaven is called ether, says Augustine, because of its flaming, and not, as Aristotle believes, because of the swiftness of its motion. The word empyrean means fiery; it indeed is fire, always moving, as we prove in *Physical Questions*. Since fire cannot be inactive, Averroes declares that when individual motion ceased, [the fiery] heaven moved in a circle. Thus Plotinus wrote in *Enneads*, II, as well as Zenocrates and Porphyrius in their answer to Aristotle's opinion that by nature fire rests in her sphere, but contrary to nature, is turned in revolution by heaven. The empyrean, or fire, cannot therefore rightly be separated from the starry heaven, which more than any other part is vigorous with fire and manifest light. In the case of that [which is said to be] placed above the starry heaven, we do not know whether it shines, much less if it is hot. Its light may not reach us, and [if it does] is perhaps only an appearance.

Because of this reason Basil does not believe it certain that such an interpretation can be substantiated, and treats the Firmament as a composition of air. This is an excellent evasion of the controversy, but it does not explain satisfactorily the text of Moses. There are no waters above the cloud-filled air except vapor which has risen from the earth. But vapor is not water, although water may be generated from it. Indeed, if vapor be generated from air, as Saint Thomas and Aristotle maintain, by what means are the fountains in the depths of the earth generated from air? Therefore according to Thomas and Aristotle, Moses does not place actual waters above the Firmament, but material from which water can no more be produced than can air and fire. The Firmament does not divide the waters from the waters, but separates any place whatsoever from any other place whatsoever, and anything you will may be conceived howsoever you will, with designating words abused, and firewood called fire and vapor called water, *et cetera*. It will be generation (not transmutation or segregation), as is taught by the ancients whom Aristotle and Saint Thomas condemn (concerning whose beliefs see our *Physical Questions* and *Metaphysics*). Again, watery vapor does not exist above solid air, but rather within the solid air itself, so that solid air does not divide the waters from the waters. Those who make heaven diaphanous, and for that reason similar to water and crystal, are pressed by a like inconsistency, for the similitude is not sufficiently complete to permit heaven to be called what the word *water* proper signifies. The air and the Sun are diaphanous, but not because they are watery. This is a false interpretation, and has no foundation in the authority of Scripture. It arises from the difficulty incurred when we do not desire to expound Moses according to Pythagorean philosophy, but rather according to the Aristotelian and Plotinian. Plato subscribed to Pythagorean beliefs; Plotinus merely constructed the natural heaven from fire. [48]

Unless the stars are regarded as worlds in which there are natural waters, as there are in the earth, the solution brought forward of actual but frozen waters above the Firmament lacks weight. For the reason that its atmosphere and waters reflect light, the earth appears to its celestial neighbours as a star among other stars, just as the Moon appears to us. It would in addition be a marvel that despite the fire in heaven the frozen waters stand fixed in systematic order, and neither melt nor dissolve within the fire, a miracle which Augustine does not allow. He was puzzled, and Basil also, but thought a better explanation could not be devised. But those who attempt to explain the text of Moses by the opinion of Aristotle are far more absurd, as Saint Thomas himself acknowledges. He regards as irrefutable the initial argument against Aristotle, if six natural days are understood as the time of the creation, and not angelic days, as believe Chrysostom, Bede, Jerome, Origen, Gregory, Ambrose, Basil, Procopius, and all the Fathers except Augustine. Yet Aristotle is harmonized with Moses only with great difficulty, even if an-

gelic days are understood. Do we not therefore condemn all the
Fathers of ignorance and impiety when we permit the impossible,
the contradictory and the false by defending Aristotle and placing
him in the Cathedral of Christ above holy teachers? Away with
such impious action and fatuous blindness!

If the waters are regarded as immaterial, only by equivocation
is it possible both to follow Aristotle and in any manner to place
them above heaven. But this practice of equivocation was ex-
ploded by all the Fathers, and if we desire to be Christians rather
than Aristotelians, it now is necessary to interpret *corporeal* in
but one sense. The Hebrew Rabbis support our position, and likewise the Pythagorean philosophers, to say nothing of Basil, Ambrose, and all Fathers and scholastics. Because he esteemed so
little both the theories and the solutions proposed by the Fathers,
Saint Thomas opposed them. He declared it impossible for vapor
to be raised from the earth above the starry heaven, regardless
of whether heaven be of fire or of the fifth essence. He also regarded this as out of the question if heaven should be of the
nature of the four elements, first, because of the distance from
earth to the starry heavens, and secondly, because vapor is
changed in that state and does not consist of minute particles of
water (except in the opinion of Anaxagoras and Empedocles,
which we discuss elsewhere). If we must follow the hypothesis
of those who believe the waters above the Firmament are elevated vapor, it is sufficient to raise vapor from the stars themselves, should they be composed of four elements as is our earth.

Notwithstanding what Saint Thomas adds from Augustine
in behalf of Aristotle, his intrepretation is not satisfactory. Moses
does not divide primary substance by the Firmament, but as all
the Fathers testify, he divides true waters. Such an interpretation makes David speak absurdly when he says, "Who coverest
the highest rooms thereof with water"; that is, the primary substance covereth heaven, and later, "Let the waters above the
heavens praise the name of the Lord." [49] In what manner
does being [*ens*] which is shapeless and virtually nothing give
praise to God, unless it either be a rational self, as the aqueous
angels of Origen, or a thing ornamented beyond measure with

beauty which manifests the excellence of God, and as Basil explains, is said to praise by a poetic figure of speech. Moreover, what miracle does Moses narrate or what wonder does he describe when he divides waters from waters by the Firmament, if the Firmament is composed of substance? It also is clear that the things under the Firmament are true waters, as we find in the sea, and for this reason those above it are of such a nature. The division is between things of the same kind, and not between a line [extension] and whiteness [color]. When therefore Saint Thomas favors the belief of Empedocles, because from him the meaning of Christian Scripture becomes intelligible, this interpretation appears to have been added because of the reticence of the Bible, to the end that Scripture should satisfy the doctors and philosophers and overflow with many meanings.

It is patent that not only Moses favors Empedocles and Galileo, but also Solomon and experience. Solomon says in Proverbs 7, "When he established the sky [ether] above, and with a certain law enclosed the depths, and poised the fountains of the waters." Because of its flaming, Augustine and Porphyrius called the ether the starry heaven. The gulfs are immense bodies of the waters, and we are not forbidden to understand that there are such bodies enclosed in many systems, since they would be contained by the earths, as our sea by our earth, and not by a ficticious congelation. The poised fountains of the waters perhaps are those in the stars, with each celestial system having its own fountain in its center. I know there are other interpretations of Solomon's text, but they were advanced prior to [Galileo's] discovery of actual appearances. Indeed, cloudy spots which manifestly could not be raised from our earth move about the Sun. Similarly, a new star in the chair of Cassiopeia was created from vapors in the year 1572, without parallax, as Tycho and innumerable mathematicians have written. Therefore there are vapors in the stars. As instruments prove, comets also occur above the Moon, which Aristotle denied. The vapors from our earth could not be carried to them, so that waters and lands [must] exist in the stars. Since other comets [composed of water] were observed near other stars, and the minute drops of vapor which Augustine and Ambrose elevated could not be raised from our earth, these comet-producing vapors proceed from the earths among the stars.

According to the Apostle Peter the heavens will be dissolved by heat, and according to David will grow old and perish. But if they are composed of the fifth essence or of fire alone, this interpretation is not tenable, unless we torture the meaning of Scripture. Saint Clement, Hilary, Cotherinus, and Augustine believe the superior heaven is immutable, [50] but not the aery heaven; therefore they differ with Aristotle. Galileo demonstrates the existence of mountains in the Moon, and Genesis 49 and Deuteronomy mention fruit trees, mountains and hills in the heavens, so that these things are appropriate for heaven. Interpreted literally, Sacred Scripture embraces in its text all meanings, including those neither mystical nor distorted, as well as the interpretation of Empedocles. Like Galileo, Empedocles was a Pythagorean. We therefore should praise Galileo, who after many centuries has by sensory experiments rescued Scripture from ridicule and distortion. He demonstrates that the wise of the world were foolish, that they should be obedient to Sacred Scripture, and not, as so long has been the fashion, that Holy Scripture should bow before them. Nor should they debase our home. Men indeed were made higher than the stars by the man Christ, and greater than the heavens. The truth gleams forth that we are more noble than they.

RESPONSE TO THE NINTH ARGUMENT AGAINST GALILEO

I deny the consequence of the ninth argument. Galileo does not conceive of the existence of a plurality of worlds, but of all worlds or systems existing under one and within one immense heaven. Indeed, [various] theologians believe there are three worlds, which by Saint Basil and Clement are described as the elementary, the celestial, and the super-celestial. Philo, Josephus, Clement of Alexandria, Jerome, and Sixtus Senensis show that the triple tabernacle of Moses was fabricated in their likeness. Galileo discusses nothing which pertains to theology, but by his marvelous instrument describes distant stars, once unknown, but now manifest. He discloses moons similar to planets which receive light from their particular sun, globes revolving about other globes, mutation of elements in heaven, and clouds above the surface of the stars, together with many newly discovered systems. This he does so that our hearts throb over the handiwork, and we declare there has returned the Moses of the Heaven of heavens, of the waters and mountains, and other things within the stars. We know that Scripture is explained according to its meaning without violence and torture and false imaginations. It has been vindicated from the calumnies of philosophers who, because they did not believe it, were driven to revert to mystical interpretations; just as the Persians now are driven to utter heresies in expounding Mohammed's impossible fictions of heaven and of divine things.

It is known that there cannot be found in the canons of the Church a decree which prohibits [belief in] a plurality of worlds. When Saint Thomas discusses this doctrine in the *Summa Theologica,* I, question 47, article 3, he does not say it is contrary to faith. The passage in John [1], "The world was made by him," [51] does not deny that other worlds and other ages were made by God; it only affirms that our own world was made by him. Saint Thomas rightly proves that to assert the existence of many worlds all without order, as did Epicurus and Democritus, is an error in faith. It follows from their opinion that the worlds were created by chance, in any fashion whatsoever, without the government of God. But to place many small systems within one great system ordained by God is by no means contrary to Scripture; it is only contrary to Aristotle. The objection of Saint Thomas, that there could not be other earths in other universes because these earths would move to our earth and lose their places, was taken from Aristotle, 1 *De Caelo,* and is not valid. My heart would not move to the place of yours. All things remain fixed in their own centers, and are preserved by and rejoice in the great similarity of their own parts. Lunary things strive to reach the center of the Moon; the mercurial, the center of Mercury. Beyond their own orb they find nothing so pleasing to them. And if the stars have the same nature, as the Aristotelians say, for this reason they do not move toward each other, but the parts of one move to it.

The articles promulgated by the University of Paris include among the errors to be corrected in Saint Thomas the proposition that another earth could not exist. This proposition limits and restricts the power of God. They also state truly that theological discourse is not concerned with natural but rather with divine things. However, Saint Thomas did not regard the power of God as circumscribed by this proposition from Aristotelian philosophy, or, as he was obliged to do if he so believed, does not say he considered this power completely restricted. As Cajetan likewise noted, Saint Thomas presents in another place the conclusion that God is able to create many worlds and earths. When he examines the discussion of Aristotle in 1 *De Coelo,* he teaches that the doctrine of a plurality of worlds is not contrary to faith but contrary to Aristotle. Moreover, the beliefs that many species of men may exist in the universe and that Christ perhaps died in other places do not follow from Galileo's statements. Nor may these beliefs be urged as the necessary consequence of others advanced by him. It is not true that if there be antipodes, Christ was again crucified in the opposite hemisphere. Yet because of this argument Augustine and many theologians denied antipodes, and opposed what present experience demonstrates to be true.

If the inhabitants which may be in other stars are men, they did not originate from Adam and are not infected by his sin. Nor do these inhabitants need redemption, unless they have committed some other sin. I am constrained to set forth those passages in Ephesians 1 ["To re-establish all things in Christ, that are in heaven and on earth"], and Colossians 1, "And through him to reconcile all things unto himself, making peace through the blood of his cross, both as to the things that are on earth, and the things that are in heaven." In his *Epistle* on the solar spots Galileo expressly denies that men [52] can exist in other stars (as I prove with scientific argument in *Physical Questions*), but affirms that beings of a higher nature can exist there. Their nature is similar to ours, but it is not the same, despite whatever sportful and jocose thing Kepler says at such length in his prefatory dissertation to the *Starry Messenger*.

Should the doctrine of a plurality of worlds be false, the conclusions of Galileo are not affected. He does not demonstrate by imagination but by sensory observation, and discloses not a plurality of worlds but many systems ordered together in one world. [Because he conceives of only one world,] Aristotle's argument in 12 *Metaphysics* against many prime movers is not pertinent. Moreover, Cardinal Cusanus, Kepler, Nolanus [Bruno], and others said the same prior to Galileo. Nor may we assume the doctrine of a plurality of worlds is untrue because the Scripture of God passes it over in silence, for argument from negative authority is false in logic. Because Scripture says nothing of antipodes, should we follow the atheists who therefore condemn Moses for his failure to speak concerning them, and have severely rebuked Augustine because for this reason he denied their existence? By such logic we could say with Luther that Peter had never been in Rome, because Luke does not mention this in the Acts. The absurd and ignorant babblers therefore may be correct. It is obvious how far removed from the insanity of Paracelsus is the doctrine of Galileo. But I am not concerned with this point. My interest is that Moses passed these doctrines in silence because he gave laws to our earth, and did not wish to discuss the physical nature of the entire universe. Yet this world is not truly our world until more of the book has been read.

Response to the Tenth Argument

In answer to the tenth argument I deny that disruptive scandal—the one thing prohibited by the Gospel—proceeds from Galileo. He does not invite this prohibited thing, but seeks to pursue truth. God commands and desires that we seek it, as is demonstrated in the second hypothesis of Chapter III, and by the passage in Scripture where Christ forbids under heavy punishment the burial of the talent. Saint Gregory says in his commentary on Ezekiel that "If scandal develops because of truth, it is desirable that we permit scandal to be born, for by it truth will be left remaining." When Christ scandalized the Pharisees, he declared in Matthew 15, "Let them alone; they are blind and leaders of the blind." It is in addition error, not to say heresy, to state that Aristotle's interpretation of the heavens and construction of the world was accepted by the scholastics as a doctrine which conformed to theology, and that they labored no further. [53] As I show in the second hypothesis and in the responses to arguments one and eight, all the Fathers oppose Aristotle's opinion regarding the heavens and the fabric of the world. The scholastics, of whom the chief are Peter Lombard and Saint Thomas, openly declare that in such things the dogmas of Aristotle cannot compare with the doctrines of Moses and the Fathers. This I pointed out in responding to arguments two and eight, and in other passages in the present discourse. The discoveries of Galileo harmonize with Holy Scripture, and rescue it from the scorn of philosophers and distortion of theologians. They demonstrate that philosophers are fallacious and their opinion less true than the testimony of the Fathers. I do not know why any person should be permitted to make men blind. Neither do I understand why one who is lacking in sound doctrine should be allowed to rage with false zeal, or lacking honest zeal, to impugn the testimony of the senses.

RESPONSE TO THE ELEVENTH ARGUMENT AGAINST GALILEO

My reply to the eleventh argument is presented complete in the first assertion of the second hypothesis and its corollary, wherein I said it is pleasing to God for man to philosophize in his book. I declared it not in vain to inquire concerning the heavens, but that such inquiry is useful to demonstrate the glory of God and to enlarge both faith in immortality and the divinity of the human soul. It was shown that the verses of Cato which attack those who scan the heavens are less weighty than the verses of Ovid, and that although David did not regard astronomy as the highest study, he commended it as sublime. I add that the argument of Cato, "He who is mortal should concern himself with mortal things," is opposed to Catholic faith. We should be concerned not only for the body but also for the soul. If indeed the soul is immortal and God-like, it scarcely will be made alienate by inquiry into divine things. Because it will not David said, "Seek the Lord, and your soul shall live"; elsewhere, "Seek his face evermore," and declared of the heavens, "The heavens show forth the glory of God," *et cetera;* "When I behold thy heavens," and again, "Wonderful are thy works, and my soul hath searched." That our Fathers did not circumscribe inquiry concerning the heavens is set forth in assertions two and three of the second hypothesis. I show in assertion four how he errs who forbids further search and in what manner wisdom leads to sobriety. But our theology abounds with illlustrations of these things.

CHAPTER V

The Arguments Presented for Galileo in the Second Chapter

I believe the arguments proposed in behalf of Galileo can now be answered only with difficulty. For many years I regarded heaven as fire, itself the fountain of all fire, and the stars to be constituted of fire, which Augustine, Basil, and other Fathers had maintained, and recently our Telesio. I also attempted in the *Physical Questions* and *Metaphysics* to refute all the arguments of Copernicus and the Pythagoreans. Yet, after the observations of Tycho and Galileo proved conclusively that new stars are in the heavens, comets are above the Moon, and that spots move about the Sun, I suspected all stars are not composed of fire. The waxing and waning of Venus and the Moon, and the spots on the Moon and Jupiter greatly strengthened this suspicion. My doubt again was increased by the argument, in contrast to what we had been taught, that the sphere of the fixed stars could not traverse so many thousand miles in a single moment. The Medicean and Saturnian stars which move about Jupiter and Saturn permit neither a single Sun; nor one center of love, that is, the Sun; and another of hate, that is, the earth; as we say in natural philosophy. Finally, the similarity of many external qualities of the fixed stars to the external qualities of the planets caused me to consider carefully the opinion which Galileo and others hold regarding [the position of] the Sun. Under these conditions I suspend my decision. I now reply to the arguments advanced for Galileo, ready to obey the commands and superior judgment of the Church.

Response to the First, Second, Third, Fourth, Fifth, and Seventh Arguments in Behalf of Galileo

I give the same answer to these arguments: the hypothesis of Copernicus and Galileo is probable, not true. For the reason that the hypothesis is not a conclusion established by the General Council of the Church, such a reply has the approval of all theologians. Neither was the theory affirmed by the Supreme Pontiff, Paul III, under the guidance of the Holy Spirit. He merely gave permission that the *Revolutions* of Copernicus might be printed, as if the hypothesis presented in the book was not repugnant to faith. [55] The Pope indeed does not approve even the doctrines of sanctified theologians in the same fashion as he approves doctrines of faith, but rather as things profitable and worthy to be read. The doctors of Paris so teach in the articles wherein they censured Saint Thomas. Were this not the case, Pope Gelasius would have confirmed the errors of Cyprian, Jerome, and the many others whom he sustains and approves in distinction fifteen of his *Catalogue* of the works of the Fathers. I also say it is probable, but not necessary, that an hypothesis is compatible with Scripture because it was announced with Papal permission and supported by the authority of concurring theologians. Nevertheless, the traducers of Galileo do not know what a present-day theologian easily may know, particularly if, as I propose in this essay, he diligently and intelligently observes heaven and the Scripture, or receives a new Revelation. I must confess I do not understand how destruction of the authority of Holy Scripture will result from the doctrines of Galileo. On the contrary, as the proverb shows, to inquire is to find riches.

Response to the Eighth, Ninth, and Tenth Arguments

I reply to these arguments that I do not know whether the conclusions advanced support Galileo, for theologians evade them by equivocal heavens and by mystical interpretaions of Scripture, as is manifest in Saint Thomas. But the evidence assembled against Aristotle cannot be questioned. We have examined in the responses for Galileo all the arguments which theologians have set forth, and truly believe Scripture favors his interpretation not less than it favors those found in the works of other philosophers. His conclusions are better presented for acceptance by the understanding. In the *Metaphysics*, I, 3, we analyzed the doctrine of Galileo and the Pythagoreans, and answered its arguments as best we might. The same was done in the *Physical Questions*, where we brought together in detail extensive evidence from nature against Copernicus. I now follow however the method of theology, wherein science is permitted to observe but the Church sits as the judge, and inquire whether Galileo should be allowed to write and to discuss his hypothesis.

RESPONSE TO THE SIXTH ARGUMENT IN BEHALF OF GALILEO

I do not know what I may deny in the sixth argument. Pico della Mirandola gives as true history the story that Aristotle, having read or heard for the first time Moses' description of the world which the creating God had poured out at the appointed season, scorned his description as rustic and as set down without scientific demonstration. [56] According to Eusebius, Porphyrius also relates the story. In contrast with this account, Ambrose testifies that Pythagoras was of Jewish descent, although I do not recall whether in his discourses or epistles. (I do not now have the books, but remember that he so stated.) When scholars doubted him, and asked, "Pray, how could Pythagoras have been a Jew when all the Greeks describe him as from Samos" (but Samos Calabria, formerly in Greater Greece, writes Barrius Franciscanus), Saint Ambrose responded that the account had been presented in an authoritative history. His sanctity and dignity, as well as our argument, indicate that he spoke accurately.

Although Pythagoras described the angels as second gods, he called the unity of God the choice of intellectual food, emulated Moses in legislation, and taught all things by number. (He fashioned all things by number, weight, and measurement, as did Moses and Solomon in the construction of the tabernacle. Concerning these points see our *Metaphysics*.) The methods of Pythagoras likewise agree with the ordinary practices followed by the Jews. The Hebrew race originated at Samos, and in the books of the Maccabees the Spartans are said to be of the race of Abraham. At the time of Moses, Abraham, and the Judges, the Jews were dispersed through many parts of the world. According to the testimony of Laertius, Plutarch, Aristotle, and Galen, Pythagoras first announced to the Gentiles his marvelous doctrine of the motion of the earth, of the Sun in the center, and of systems in heaven. He informed them that the Moon is another earth, and that the four elements, not to mention water, exist in the stars. This doctrine appears to have been obtained from Moses, for such great wisdom could not come into being without revelation. Copernicus began to develop his system from the preceding contributions of the Pythagoreans, motivated by the observations of Francesco Maria. The disciple of Pythagoras, our Timaeus Locrus, demonstrated by mathematics the diurnal rotation of the earth, and Philolaus of Crotona the annual revolution. As I show in *Physical Questions,* Copernicus then added the motion of libration from the pattern of the motion devised by Thebit of Babylon and King Alfonso of Spain. That such a motion was necessary Saint Thomas also suggested in 12 *Metaphysics* from the statements of Simplicius.

If Pythagoras were not a Jew, as [Ambrose's unnamed] authority taught the father of philosophy, nevertheless we may recount true history with the Egyptian priests, with Pherecydes of Syra, and with the Jews in Judea bordering upon Syrian Egypt (itself twice turned into Syria and Egypt). From them we hear both the Law and the philosophy of waters, mountains, and earths in heaven, of mountains in the Moon and similar things, which in this question we showed are described in the Sacred Books. Moreover, Aristotle [57] derided the Hebrew Moses, and also the Hebrew or Hebraized Pythagoras. It is fitting that by infallible instruments and demonstrations, and in accord with the Apostle, we Christians and spiritual descendents of the Hebrews should vindicate the sacred Mosaic philosophy from the calumny of heretics. Why do we complain [against Galileo], much as the Jews once complained against Moses, the defender of his own from the wrongs of the Egyptians? The ancient Rabbis, whose works I now lack, teach much the same philosophy. As the ecstatic teacher, Denys the Carthusian, narrates in his books against Mohammed, the doctrine was taught by Mohammed in the dialogue with Abdia of Judea and in the Koran, as well as by the Arabs and Jews who followed him. Mohammed places many seas, mountains, and aery spaces in the heavens, and seven earths with cattle sustaining them under our earth. As Sixtus Senensis,

Denys the Carthusian, and others testify, the Hebrews and Talmudists also accepted this belief.

It is apparent from his statements that Mohammed was ignorant, and because of this uttered whatever came into his mouth just as it was caught. As he shows in his history of Joseph, David, Solomon, and Jesus Christ our Lord, he mingled truth with falsehood. He was unable to distinguish between metaphor and fact, and set up columns holding the world, and rivers of wine and milk in paradise (as they are mentioned in Job), together with other similar notions. To the end that heaven may not fall down, it is supported by a great mountain, from which it derives its somewhat greenish color. The idea of the sustaining mountain Mohammed took from the Christians who, since they considered it no part of geography, raised almost to heaven the eminence upon which they believed the earthly paradise was placed. Because of its height, Anastasius of Sinai questioned how men had descended from it. I pass over what Bede says of these things. One point alone I take from his statements: that Mohammed obtained from the Rabbis the doctrine of many earths and systems above our heaven.

Because the hypothesis of Galileo and of Empedocles (who received it from the Pythagoreans) harmonizes well with the most ancient and the modern interpretations of Holy Writ, the Sacred Scripture is in accord with the explanation of celestial things provided by the new philosophy. According to the testimony of Saint Thomas, many thinkers other than Empedocles accepted the doctrine from the Pythagoreans. The Pythagoreans obtained the doctrine from the Jews, and with their conclusions Galileo now largely agrees. [58] He was not influenced to do so by unsubstantial opinion, but by valid sensory observation. As I show in the second hypothesis. I therefore believe with Saint Thomas and Augustine that we cannot spurn sublime genius without bringing ridicule upon Scripture, or raising the strong suspicion that with atheists we believe contrary to its Sacred Word. Bellarmine himself declares that at this time heretics do not endanger Roman theology, and for this reason alone it is unnecessary that the investigations of Galileo should be forbid-

den and his books suppressed, a misfortune which is about to
occur. Our enemies will seize eagerly upon this action, and pro-
claim it abroad.

. . . . . .

In the above statements, discussions, and writings I at all
times submit myself to the correction and better judgment of our
Holy Mother the Roman Church. Farewell most illustrious Cardinal Gaetani, protector of Italian excellence.

F I N I S.

NOTES

The page cited preceding each note is that of the Frankfort edition (1622) of the *Defense*, as indicated by brackets above or within the text. Where individuals are referred to by Campanella in more than one instance, the note on the initial reference normally includes explanatory data for those which follow. The most convenient source for compact biographies of the Fathers and other churchmen is the *Catholic Encyclopedia*, which concludes each life with an adequate general bibliography. The works of the more important Fathers will be found in the Greek or Latin series of Migne's *Patrologiae*. The histories, biographies, and special articles cited in the Introduction may be supplemented either by the following or by similar works.

Bredvold, Louis I., "The Religious Thought of Donne in Relation to Medieval and Later Traditions," *Studies in Shakespeare, Milton and Donne* . . . , New York, 1925, pp. 193-232.

Burke, R. B., ed., *The Opus Majus of Roger Bacon*, 2 vols., Philadelphia, 1928.

Burtt, E. A., *The Metaphysical Foundations of Modern Phyiscal Science*, New York, 1925.

Collier, Katherine B., *Cosmogonies of Our Fathers*, New York, 1934.

Curry, Walter Clyde, *Chaucer and the Mediaeval Sciences*, New York, 1926.

Dampier-Whetham, W. C., *A History of Science*, Cambridge, 1929.

Gilson, E., *The Philosophy of Saint Thomas Aquinas*, 1929.

————— *The Spirit of Medieval Philosophy*, 1936.

Haskins, C. H., *Studies in the History of Mediaeval Science*, 2nd ed., Cambridge, Mass., 1927.

Husik, Isaac, *A History of Medieval Jewish Philosophy*, New York, 1916.

McIntyre, J. L., *Giordano Bruno*, London, 1903.

McKeon, R., *The Philosophy of Spinoza*, 1928.

Menon, C. P. S., *Early Astronomy and Cosmology*, London, 1932.

Munk, S., *Mélanges de Philosophie Juive et Arabe*, Paris (1857), 1927.

Neumark, David, *Geschichte der jüdischen Philosophie des Mittelalters*, 2 vols., Berlin, 1907.

Ornstein, Martha, *The Rôle of Scientific Societies in the Seventeenth Century*, 2nd ed., Chicago, 1928.

Patrick, M. M., *The Greek Sceptics*, 1929.

Pouchet, F. A., *Histoire des Sciences Naturelles au Moyen Âge*, Paris, 1853.

Rashdall, Hastings, *The Universities of Europe in the Middle Ages*, ed. Powicke and Emden, 3 vols., Oxford, 1936.

Renan, Ernest, *Averroes et l'Averroïsme*, 4th ed., Paris, 1882.

Robbins, F. E., *The Hexaemeral Literature*, Chicago, 1912.

Ross, W. D., *Aristotle*, 1924.

Singer, Charles, and others, *Studies in the History and Method of Science*, Oxford, 1921.

Smith, Preserved, *A History of Modern Culture: The Great Renewal, 1543-1687*, New York, 1930.

Simpson, James Y., *Landmarks in the Struggle between Science and Religion*, New York, 1926.

Stimson, Dorothy, *The Gradual Acceptance of the Copernican Theory of the Universe*, New York, 1917.

Taylor, Henry Osborn, *The Mediaeval Mind*, 2 vols., New York, 1919.

————— *Thought and Expression in the Sixteenth Century*, New York, 1920.

Thomson, J. A., *Science and Religion*, New York, 1925.

Thorndike, Lynn, *A History of Magic and Experimental Science during the First Thirteen Centuries of Our Era*, 2 vols., New York, 1929; *Fourteenth and Fifteenth Centuries*, 2 vols., New York, 1934.

———— *Science and Thought in the Fifteenth Century*, New York, 1929.

Vacant and Mangenot, *Dictionnaire de Théologie Catholique.*

Wolf, A., *A History of Science, Technology, and Philosophy in the Sixteenth and Seventeenth Centuries*, London, 1935.

Wolfson, Harry Austryn, tr. and ed., *Crescas' Critique of Aristotle*, Cambridge, 1929.

de Wulf, M., *History of Medieval Philosophy*, 2nd ed., 1926.

P. 3. Lyncean philosophers: The "academy" of the "Lynxes," sponsored by Prince Cesi, which met informally in Rome in the first years of the seventeenth century. Giovanni Battista Porta (*Galilei Opere* [1901], XI, 611) attributes the coinage of the word "telescope" to Prince Cesi: "Telescopium multis ostendi (lubet hoc uti nomine a meo principe reperto)." The many names applied to "Galileo's" optic tube are discussed by Professor Nicolson, "The Telescope and Imagination," *loc. cit.*, p. 245. The earliest extended scientific treatise to employ exclusively and repeatedly the term telescope is the *Sphaera Mundi* of Josephus Blancanus, or Giuseppe Biancani (1620).

P. 4. Lazzaro Scoriggio: The name also was spelled Lazzaro Scorriggio. In a third variation it is given as Leonardo Scoriggio.

———— Nicolas Hill: The author of *Philosophia Epicurea, Democritiana, Theophrastica, proposita simpliciter, non edocta*, Paris, 1601 (another edition, Geneva, 1619). In Proposition 434 of this work, Hill presented nineteen arguments in favor of the Copernican theory. He was B. A. and Fellow of St. John's College, Oxford, and at one time probably secretary to Edward De Vere, Earl of Oxford.

———— Redento Baranzano: Giovanni Antonio Baranzano, 1590-1622, professor of physics and philosophy at Annecy, opponent of Aristotle and friend of Galileo and Francis Bacon. He is said to have communicated to Bacon the theory of the *Novum Organum*. Baranzano wrote *Uranoscopia seu de Coelo . . .*, Lyon, 1617, and the unpublished *Nova de Motu Terrae Copernico . . . disputatio.*

P. 5. Cardinal Gaetani: It later became the responsibility of Cardinal Gaetani to amend the *Revolutions* of Copernicus in accordance with the decree of the Sacred Congregation, and therefore to cause the book to present the heliocentric theory as a mere hypothesis. The relatively few emendations made are reprinted by Riccioli, *op. cit.*, I, ii, 496-7.

P. 7. Psalms 92 and 103 of the Douay and modern Catholic Versions are, with minor variations, Psalms 93 and 104 of the Vulgate and American Revised Version.

P. 8. 3 Esdras 4: 3 Esdras is not included in the Vulgate or modern Catholic version of Scripture. Its equivalent will be found in 1 Esdras of the Apocrypha of the King James Version.

———— Martin Delrio: Martin Anton Delrio, 1551-1608, scholar, statesman, Jesuit theologian. His second work, published at the age of 23, contained citations from nearly 1100 authors. He is best known for his treatise on magic, *Disquisitionum Magicarum Libri Sex*, the work mentioned by Campanella.

———— Cato: Campanella quotes from the *Moral Distichs*, known variously as *Dicta Catonis, Dionysii Catonis Disticha de Moribus ad Filium, Parvus Cato et Magnus Cato*, etc. The distich is number 2 of Book II of the modern version, which is:

> An di sint caelum que regant, ne quaere doceri:
> Cum sis mortalis, quae sunt mortalia, cura.

In the *Parvus Cato et Magnus Cato* (tr. Benet Burgh, Westminster. 1477), whose version is similar to that used by Campanella, the distich is number 7 [unnumbered] of Book II. Campanella quotes the distich as follows:

> Mitte arcana Dei, coelumque inquirere quid sit,
> Cum sis mortalis, quae sunt mortalia, cura.

P. 9. Pope Paul III: Alessandro Farnese, 1468-1549; elected 12 October, 1534. As Dean of the Sacred College of Cardinals, Paul III spent his immense revenue in assisting learned men and the people of Rome. Seven sessions of the Council of Trent (13 December, 1545—3 March, 1547) were held during his Pontificate. Before its disruption by the plague, the Council formulated "for all time" the Catholic doctrine on the Scripture, original sin, justification, and the Sacrament.

———— Cardinal Schonberg: Nicolaus Cardinal von Schonberg, Archbishop of Capua, and trusted councillor of both Clement VII and Paul III, who wrote in 1536 to Copernicus, entreating him to make known his discovery to the world, and requesting a transcript of the *Revolutions* and its tables, to be copied at his expense.

———— John Stadius: Author of the *Ephemerides Novae* (1556), based upon the *Tabulae Prutenicae* which Erasmus Reinhold had in large measure constructed from the tables in the *Revolutions* of Copernicus. As I point out in "An Early Friend of the Copernican *Theory: Gemma Frisius,*" *Isis,* XXVI (1937), 322-5, the prefatory letter from Gemma to Stadius which opens the *Ephemerides Novae* is one of the earliest commendations of Copernican astronomy to be made subsequent to publication of the *Revolutions*.

———— Francesco Maria of Ferrara: Domenico Maria da Novara, 1454-1504. During the three and one-half years which Copernicus spent at the University of Bologna he was closely associated with Novara, a practical astronomer of some standing. In contrast with Campanella's statement that Copernicus was a disciple of Novara, Rheticus declared (*Narratio Prima,* ed. cit., p. 448) his association was "rather as a friend and assistant than as a pupil." Dreyer (*History,* p. 307) believes the example of Novara "probably encouraged Copernicus to watch the heavens," but concludes "however useful the acquaintance with . . . [him] may have been . . . we may take it for granted that neither he nor any other Italian savant sowed the seed which eventually produced the fruit known as the Copernican System." Dreyer's conclusion is of course an assumption.

Pp. 9-10. (Nor were the heretics . . . their books): The parentheses are not in the text.

P. 10. Clavius: Christoph Clau, 1538-1612, Jesuit mathematician and astronomer whose greatest work was assistance rendered in the reform of the calendar under Gregory XIII. His *Commentary* on Sacro Bosco virtually dominated the field for three decades after 1581. Among his noted pupils were Griemberger and Blancanus (Biancani).

———— Saint Ambrose: C. 340-397, bishop of Milan from 374 to 397, and one of the most illustrious Fathers and Doctors of the Church. His *Hexaemeron* and other scripture-commentaries deal with the story of Creation, the Old Testament figures of Cain and Abel, Abraham and the patriarchs, David and the Psalms, and related subjects. His hymns indicate his mastery of the Latin language.

———— Giovanni Pico della Mirandola: 1463-1494, Italian theologian, philosopher and scholar, celebrated pupil of Marsilio Ficino, Platonist and cabbalist. *Cf.* Sandys, *A History of Classical Scholarship,* Cambridge. 1908. II. 82 ff.

P. 11. Caselli: Tommaso Caselli, Dominican of the middle of the 16th century, who lived in the diocese of Bertino, province of Forli, Italy. He is known as an able theologian.

———— Saint Justin: Justin Martyr, c. 100-165, Saint and Christian apologist. Two apologies bearing his name, and his *Dialogue with the Jew Tryphon* have been preserved. The first *Apology* apparently is organized so as to show the weakness of Aristotle, Plato, the Pythagorean and other pagan philosophers, and to contrast their teaching with that of Christ and the Prophets.

———— Saint Bernard: Bernard of Clairvaux, 1090-1153, Order of St. Benedict. Among his works are the *Apology to William of St. Thierry, against the Claims of the Monks of Cluny,* to which Campanella refers, and *Homilies on the Gospel "Missus est."*

P. 12. Antipodes: The early Fathers objected to antipodes, or inhabitants on the opposite side of the earth, because they believed no inhabitants of the known world could have travelled around the earth. As they reasoned, these inhabitants therefore could not have descended from Adam. Scripture seemingly was questioned, and, as some believed, the "antipodes" could only be saved by a second crucifixion. In the year 748 Virgilius was removed from his bishopric and excommunicated for believing either in antipodes or in another world under the earth. Caesar Baronius (*Annales Ecclesiastici,* Lucae, 1742, XII, 551) states that Virgilius held the latter belief. It seems probable however that he supported the former. Cf. H. Vander Linden, "Virgile de Salsbourg et les Théories Cosmographique au VIII Siècle," Académie Royale de Belgique, *Bulletin* . . . , Bruxelles, 1914 (Lettres, IV, 163 ff.).

———— Pope Leo: Apparently Leo I (The Great), Saint, ?-461. Except for that of St. Gregory I, Leo's pontificate (440-61) is regarded as the most significant and important in Christian antiquity. His principal aim was to keep the Church unified. He attacked heresy vigorously, and on several occasions warned the Christians of Rome against the Manichaeans, urging that they disclose to the authorities the names, addresses and meeting places of these heretics.

P. 13. Saint Thomas: Thomas Aquinas, 1225 or 1227-1274, Saint, philosopher, theologian, doctor of the Church (Angelicus Doctor), patron of Catholic universities, colleges and schools, and the greatest of the scholastics. Campanella cites the following works by Saint Thomas:

    (a) *De Coelo,* a commentary on *De Caelo* of Aristotle. In this work Saint Thomas employs "lectio" in place of "caput." I cite "lectio" as "chapter."

    (b) *Opusculum contra Errores Graecorum,* translated as *Tract Against the Errors of the Greeks.*

    (c) *Opusculum contra Impugnantes Religionem,* an apology for the religious orders, referred to as the *Reply.* This work challenges *De Periculis Novissimorum Temporum* of William of St. Amour, which attacked the friars and denied their right to occupy chairs in the University of Paris. As the result of Thomas's *Reply* (1256), the Pope ordered that mendicant friars should be admitted to the doctorate.

    (d) *Summa de Veritate Catholicae Fidei contra Gentiles,* cited as *Treatise on the Truth of the Catholic Faith, against Unbelievers.*

    (e) *Summa Theologica,* a detailed and organized exposition of theology and summary of Christian philosophy. The *Summa* is divided into four divisions: Part I; Part II, first part; Part II, second part, and Part III. It is customary at present to cite the second division as II, i; and the third as II, ii. Campanella cites the first part of Part II as II. He does not mention the *Summa* by title, and on occasion omits the article (of the question) referred to. I have supplied the articles except where his reference is to the question, *passim.*

———— Albertus Magnus: Albert the Great, of Swabia, (?1193) 1205 or 1206-1280, scientist, philosopher and theologian, and instructor of

Saint Thomas, whose teachings he defended in Paris (1277) against
Bishop Stephen Tempier and others. He was beatified by Pope
Gregory XV in 1622. I venture the judgment that Albertus was the
most influential neo-Aristotelian of the 13th century. He was in addition one of its most important "scientists."

—— Avicenna: Abn Ali al Hosain Ibn Abdullah Ibn Sina, 980-1037,
Arabian physician and philosopher. His philosophy is based upon
Aristotle and neo-Platonism. Avicenna's favorite principle, that the
universality of our ideas is the result of the activity of the mind itself,
was quoted by Averroes, the scholastics, and especially by Albertus.
He wrote the famous "Canon" of medical science.

—— Saint Ephrem: Ephraem, Ephrem, Ephraim, early 4th century-373,
wrote in Syriac commentaries on the entire Scripture. There are extant his commentary on Genesis and an extended portion of that on
Exodus.

—— Anastasius of Sinai: Anastasius Sinaita, 1st half of 7th century-d.
after 700, Saint, Greek ecclesiastical writer, and abbot of the mon-
astery of Mt. Sinai. His principal works are the *Hodegos* or *Guide*,
and *Introduction to the Hexaemeron*, twelve books, the first eleven of
which are extant in a Latin translation.

—— Moses, Bishop of Syria: Moses bar Cephas, c. 813-903, Syriac
bishop and writer, whose works include commentaries on Old and
New Testaments. A MS. copy of his *Hexaemeron* in five books is
preserved in the Bibliothèque Nationale, Paris. He wrote a commentary on Aristotle's *Dialectica*, now lost, and a treatise against heretics.

—— Terence: The text is, "Et poeta Comicus de tali iudice ait:
    Dij immortales, homine imperito nihil iniustius,
    Qui nil rectum, nisi quod placeat sibi ducit."
Campanella either quoted the *Adelphi*, I, 98-9, from memory or employed a text unlike the modern, which reads:
    Homine imperito numquam quicquam iniustius,
    Qui nisi quod ipse fecit nil rectum putat.

P. 14. Lateran Council under Leo X: Leo X, Giovanni de Medici,
1475-1521, Pope, 1513-21. He continued the Fifth Lateran Council
begun under Julius II, 19 April, 1512. The final session was held 16
March, 1517. One of Leo's decrees condemned "the false philosophical
teachings" of Pietro Pomponazzi, professor at Padua, who denied the
immortality of the soul. A second decree, issued 2 May, 1515, forbade
under pain of excommunication the printing of books without permission of the ordinary of the diocese. The reputation of Leo rests upon
his personal interest in literature, science, and art.

P. 15. Augustine: Augustine of Hippo, 354-430, Saint, Doctor of the
Church, the object of whose philosophy is to provide for theology
the support of reason. In his great commentary on Genesis, *De Genesi
ad Literam*, I, 19 and 21, especially n. 39, he reiterates that Christians
must be on their guard against setting forth interpretations of Scripture which are hazardous or opposed to science, and thereby exposing
Holy Writ to the ridicule of unbelievers.

—— Jerome: Saint, c. 341-420, most famous of the ancient exegetes,
who indulged in various theological controversies and wrote numerous
commentaries on Scripture, historical works, and translations, and
letters. Saint Jerome maintained there is in the Bible no material
error occasioned by the ignorance or carelessness of the writer, but
added (*Pat. Lat.*, XXVI, 98; XXIX, 855) that it is customary for
the sacred historian to conform himself to the generally accepted
opinion of the vulgar of his day. His correspondence (*ibid.*,
XXII-XXX) is the best known of his literary work.

—— Dionysius: Bishop of Alexandria from 247-8 to 264-5, named "the
Great" by Eusebius, St. Basil, and others, one of the most eminent

bishops of the third century. He usually wrote in the form of letters. His treatise in connection with the apocalypse is regarded as a noteworthy example of higher criticism.

—— Gregory: Gregory I (the Great), c. 540-604, Saint, Pope (590-604), Doctor of the Church, one of the most important figures in ecclesiastical history, who definitely affected the doctrine, organization, and discipline of the Catholic Church. Two of his more important works are *Moralium Libri XXXV*, cited by Campanella, and *Regulae Pastoralis Liber*.

—— Chrysostom: John Chrysostom (John the golden-mouthed), c. 347-407, Saint, the most important Doctor of the Greek Church, and the greatest pulpit orator of the Catholic. His works fall into the three divisions of "opuscula," "homilies," and "letters." The principal commentaries on the Old Testament are the sixty-seven homilies "On Genesis"; those on the New Testament, the numerous homilies on Matthew, John and the Acts. The thirty-four homilies on the Epistle to the Hebrews were published posthumously.

P. 16. 3 Kings: 1 and 2 Kings of the Catholic Version are 1 and 2 Samuel of the Protestant. 3 Kings of the Catholic is 1 Kings of the Protestant.

—— Brigid: Saint Brigid of Ireland (erroneously called Bridget), c. 451-525, patroness of students and artists. A later Saint Brigit or Bridget (of Sweden) founded in 1346 the Brigittine Order.

—— Cyril: Cyril of Alexandria, fl. first third of the fifth century, Saint, Doctor of the Church, and writer of numerous exegetical works. Of the twenty books of his great apologic work against Julian the Apostate, cited by Campanella, only ten are extant.

—— Julian the Apostate: Flavius Claudius Julianus, 331-363, Roman emperor 361-3, who received a Christian training, but was moved by the murder of his relatives in a massacre to a hatred of all Christians. Until 361 Julian was outwardly a Christian, but in this year he permitted himself to be described as having the protection of Zeus, and ordered all cities to open the temples for pagan worship, including the sacrifice of animals. He decreed that all property and immunities bestowed upon the Christians by Constantine be taken away, and forbade the appointment of Christians as teachers of rhetoric and grammar.

—— Nicephorus: Saint, c. 758-829, Patriarch of Constantinople 806-815. Campanella perhaps refers to one of the seventy-five extracts from the Fathers which formed an appendix to the second part of Nicephorus' *Apology for the Pure and Unadulterated Faith of Christians against Those Who Accuse Us of Idolatry*.

—— Anthony: Saint, founder of Christian monasticism, b. middle of the third century, and d. 356-7. It has not been determined how many of the sayings attributed to him in the "Apophthegmata" are his utterances.

—— Lactantius: Lucius Caecilius Firmianus Lactantius, fl. early fourth century, an African Christian apologist whose greatest work, *The Divine Institutions (Divinarum Institutionum Libri VIII)*, 304-311, is the first attempt at a systematic exposition of Christian theology in Latin. Other works are *Epitome Divinarum Institutionum* and *De Ira Dei*.

—— Ovid: The initial quotation is from the *Metamorphoses*, I, 84-6, with the first verse given by Campanella as "Cum terram spectent animalia caetera prona." The modern text is "Pronaque cum spectent animalia cetera terram." The second quotation is from the *Fasti*, Ovid's poetical treatise on the Roman calendar, I, 297-8; 305-6. The first verse of Campanella's version employs "primum" rather than the more common "primus."

—— Axiochus: Although Marsilio Ficino had denied the *Axiochus* a place in the Platonic canon as early as 1497, it was generally attributed to Plato throughout the sixteenth century. Modern scholars regard the authorship as unknown. The question of authorship is discussed briefly by Frederick Morgan Padelford, *The Axiochus of Plato,* Baltimore, 1934, p. 16, and in greater detail by Wilhelm von Christ, *Geschichte der Griechischen Literatur,* München, 1912, p. 420 (J. von Müller, *Handbuch der Klassischen Altertums-Wissenschaft*).

P. 17. Josephus: Flavius Josephus, 37-*c.* 101, Jewish historian of a distinguished priestly family. His *History of the Jews* was frequently quoted by the Fathers and early historians of the Church.

────── Philo: Philo Judaeus (Philo the Jew), born *c.* 25 B. C., philosopher and theologian whose writings consist of apologetical works, philosophical treatises, and exposition of the Jewish law. The philosophical treatises include *On the Liberty of the Wise, On the Incorruptibility of the World, On Providence,* and a compilation of passages from other works entitled *De Mundo.*

────── Berosus: A native historian of Babylonia who flourished during and after the lifetime of Alexander the Great. He was well versed in the astronomy and astrology of his day, and is said by Vitruvius to have invented a semi-circular sundial. Campanella probably refers to his Greek history of Babylonia, entitled both *Babyloniaca* and *Chaldaica* by various writers, among them Clement of Alexandria and Josephus. The second book deals with human history from the Flood to Nabonassar.

────── Patriarch Jacob: *Cf.* Genesis 30.25 ff.

P. 18. Eccentricity: Deviation from center or from the line of a circle, as an orbit.

Apogee: The point in the orbit of a heavenly body which is (or appears to be) farthest from the earth.

Equinox: The time when the sun's center crosses the celestial equator, or about March 21 and September 22.

Acronychus: The rising or setting of any star or planet at sunset.

────── Saint Basil: Basil the Great, *c.* 329-379, Saint, Bishop of Caesarea, one of the most distinguished Doctors of the Church. In interpreting the Scripture, Basil employed both the literal and allegorical methods. The *Hexaemeron,* cited by Campanella, is one of his most influential works.

P. 19. Calippus and Eudoxus: Early Chaldean astronomy postulated seven or eight homocentric spheres. Sometime later this number was increased to ten, eventually to twelve, and in the hypothesis of Eudoxus of Cnidos to twenty-six. In order to "correct" constantly appearing discrepancies, Calippus extended the number to thirty-three and Aristotle to fifty-five, all but one of which were assigned to the several planets.

────── Thebit: Tabit ben Korra, 826-901, Arabian astronomer and prolific translator and writer best known in the history of astronomy as an advocate of the erroneous idea of the oscillatory motion of the equinoxes. In his unprinted *On the Motion of the Eighth Sphere,* he imagines in the ninth sphere a fixed ecliptic which intersects the equator in two points under an angle of 23 degrees, 33 minutes, and thirty seconds, and a moveable ecliptic in the eighth sphere attached at two diametrically opposite points to two small circles.

────── King Alfonso: Alfonso X of Castille, 1252-84, who invited astronomers to his court to assist in preparation of the famous Alfonsine Tables.

────── Eugene: Eugene III, ?-1153, Pope (1145-53), Blessed. He was deeply influenced by Saint Bernard of Clairvaux, and it was for him that Bernard wrote the handbook for popes entitled *De Consideratione* which Campanella cites.

P. 20. Richard of St. Victor: ?-1173, native of Scotland, theologian, and disciple of the mystic Hugo. In keeping with the School of St. Victor,

Richard utilized the didactic methods in theology which Abelard had introduced. He regarded secular learning as worthless if considered as an end in itself. His mystical theology is largely set forth in the two books on mystical contemplation, *Benjamin Minor* and *Benjamin Major*, to which Campanella refers.

P. 21. Saint Clement (Clemens) : Apparently Clement I, Saint, Pope, and ?fourth Bishop of Rome, called Clemens Romanus to distinguish him from the Alexandrian. He is the first of the successors of St. Peter concerning whom any definite information is available. Origen, Eusebius, and Jerome identify him as a fellow-laborer of Saint Paul. Many writings have been attributed to Saint Clement but only one, *Epistle to the Corinthians* is regarded as his. Among the pseudo-Clementine works is a letter to James which appears in many MSS. of the *Recognitions*.

───── Barnabas : Originally Joseph, Saint, named an apostle in Scripture and ranked by the Church with the Twelve. Various traditions describe him as the first Bishop of Milan, and as having preached at Rome, where he converted Pope Saint Clement.

P. 22. Since Moses was unusually learned in every field of knowledge : John Wilkins (*Discourse*, London, 1640, pp. 76-7) says of this tradition : "It has been an ancient and common opinion amongst the Jews that the Law of Moses did contain in it not only those things which concern our religion and obedience, but every secret also that may possibly be known in any art or science, so that there is not a demonstration in Geometry or rule in Arithmetic, nor a mystery in any trade, but it may be found out in the *Pentateuch*. Hence it was, say they, that Solomon had all his wisdom. . . . Nay from hence they thought a man might learne the art of miracles, to remove a mountain or recover the dead. . . . Not much unlike this foolish superstition of theirs, is that custom of many artists among us . . . ."

P. 23. Averroes : Abul Walid Mohammed Ibn Achmed, Ibn Mohammed Ibn Roschd, 1126-1198, Arabian philosopher, astronomer, and writer on jurisprudence. His commentaries on Aristotle, original philosophical works, and theological treatises are extant either in Latin or Hebrew translations. He maintained that religion has one sphere and philosophy another. The "Grand Commentary" of Ibn Roschd, or Averroes, was employed by Saint Thomas as his model for exposition. Under the Caliph Abu Jacub Jusuf, and under his son Jacub Al Mansur, he enjoyed many privileges, but later fell into disfavor, and was banished with other men of learning.

───── Alfarabius : Al Farabi, Arabian philosopher of the tenth century who wrote at length on Aristotle and attempted to reconcile Aristotelian and Platonic thought. His *Encyclopedia* was highly valued by the Christian scholastics.

───── Haly : Probably Abu 'l Hassan Ali Ben Amagiur, early tenth century, Arabian astronomer of Morocco.

───── Albumasar : Abumassar or Abu Mashar, born *c.* 805, from Balkh in Chorassan, regarded by the Middle Ages as the greatest Arabian astrologer.

P. 24. Articles condemned at Paris : Two hundred and nineteen propositions, largely Aristotelian and Averroistic, condemned in 1277 by Stephen Tempier, Bishop of Paris. They are reproduced under the title *Opiniones ducentae undeviginti . . . a Stephano episcopo Parisiensi de consilio doctorum sacrae scripturae condemnatae,* 1277, Marti 7, Parisiis, in *Chartularium Universitatis Parisiensis . . .* Collegit Henricus Denifle . . . auxiliante Æmilio Chatelain, 2 vols., Paris, 1889-1891, I, 544 ff.

───── Christ . . . in whose shackles Ecclesiasticus places our feet. Campanella seems to have equated Christ with the "wisdom . . . from the Lord God" discussed in Ecclesiasticus 1.1 ff. Ecclesiasticus will be found in the Catholic Version preceding Isaiah.

—— Antonio Mirandola: Apparently Antonio Bernardo della Mirandola, fl. 1550, Bishop of Caserta, Italy, and famous student of Aristotle.

—— The Apostle: The Apostle Paul.

P. 25. Epistle to Pammachius: Pammachius, died *c.* 409, Saint, Roman senator, who as a youth attended school with St. Jerome. When he later censured Jerome's book against Jovinian, the Saint wrote him two conciliatory letters, the first of which vindicated the book and apparently was intended for publication. A number of Jerome's Scriptural commentaries were dedicated to Pammachius.

—— *Summa Theologica*, I, question 1, articles 5 ff. Campanella's citation ("I, 1") is inaccurate, and apparently should include and emphasize the *Reply* and the *Tract* as cited p. 32. In the *Summa*, I, 1, Saint Thomas confines himself to the points that theology is the sole judge of the sciences, that it is greater than they, and that whatever in them is found repugnant to theology must be condemned as false.

—— Bembo: Probably Pietro Bembo, 1470-1547, famous Italian scholar and Cardinal, who studied philosophy under Pomponazzi at Padua and Greek under Lascaris at Messina. In time he renounced the classics and devoted himself to the Holy Scripture and the works of the Fathers.

P. 26. Machiavelli: Nicolò Machiavelli, 1469-1527, Italian statesman and historian, whose *Principe* or *The Prince* made his name synonymous with treachery, intrigue, tyranny, and disregard of all Christian principles. One of the most offensive principles is that whoever would overcome treachery and cruelty in others must deceive his enemies before they have an opportunity to play falsely with him. *The Prince* was placed on the Index in 1559, perhaps in part because it urged a united Italy.

P. 27. Cardinal Cajetan: Tommaso de Vio Gaetani (baptized Giacomo), 1469-1534, Dominican cardinal, philosopher, theologian, and exegete. As a theologian Cajetan stands as one of the foremost exponents and defenders of Thomism. His pioneer commentaries on the *Summa Theologica*, begun in 1507 and completed 1522, were immediately recognized as a classic in scholastic literature. The primary purpose of Cajetan was to defend St. Thomas against the attacks of Scotus. In his Pontifical Letters of 15 October, 1879, Leo XIII ordered Cajetan's commentaries and those of Ferrariensis incorporated with the text of the *Summa Theologica* in the official Leonine edition of the complete works of St. Thomas. Campanella refers to Cajetan's gloss on the *Summa*, I, question 1, article 10.

P. 28. Ulisse Albergotti: Campanella refers to the *Dialogue* of Albergotti, published in 1613: "Dialogo di Fr. Ulisse Albergotti Aretino Cavaliere Gerosolimitano e Commendatore di S. Pietro alla Magione di Siena; nel quale si tiene, contro l'opinione comune degli Astrologi, Matematici e Filosofi, la Luna esser da sè luminosa, e non ricevere il lume dal Sole, nè che gli ecclissi di lei si causino dall' interposizione della Terra fra questi doi luminarj, e che nè anco quelli del Sole siano causati dall' interposizione della Luna fra noi e il Sole: Interlocutori Astro et Logia. In Viterbo appresso Girolamo discepolo, anno 1613."

—— Procopius Gaza: Procopius of Gaza, sixth century, theologian and exegete, one of the first to write a catena. The early Fathers attempted above all else to reconcile the presumed facts of nature with beliefs supposed to be taught in Scripture, and because of the predominantly exegetical character of the beginnings of Christian literature, all ideas were brought into harmony with current interpretations of the Bible. Among the Fathers who declared the earth flat in accord with Scripture, and on this ground alone were in position to refute "antipodes," were Procopius, Theodore of Mopsuestia, St. John Chrysostom, and Severian of Gabala. Clement, Origen, Ambrose, Basil, and Augustine seem on the whole to have accepted the belief of Aristotle, Ptolemy, and others that the earth was spherical in shape.

——— Isidore: Isidore of Seville, c. 560-636, Saint, a voluminous writer whose compositions have been said to constitute the first chapter of Spanish literature. His most important work is the *Origines,* or *Etymologiae,* a condensed and ordered exposition of the greater part of the learning possessed by his day. The *Etymologies* became one of the most popular textbooks of the Middle Ages. Similar in general character is the *Libri duo differentiarum,* the first book of which is entitled *De Differentiis Verborum* and the second, *De Differentiis Rerum.* A third work, *De Natura Rerum,* treats astronomy, geography and miscellaneous topics. This was perhaps the best known of Isidore's books during the Middle Ages; in any event it enjoyed an unusually wide popularity.

——— Xenophanes: Born at Colophon, near Ephesus. A large part of his life was spent in Sicily, where he died about the middle of the fifth century, B. C., at the age of ninety-two. His philosophy, or theology, suggests monotheism, and held that there is only one God who is unlike men in form and thought. This deity "sees over all, thinks over all, and hears over all." The world is through and through thinking and animate.

P. 29. Bishop Philastrius: Saint, Bishop of Brescia, d. before 397. His catalogue of heresies, *Diversarum Hereseon Liber,* to which Campanella alludes, was composed about 384. As a priest, he travelled over most of the Roman world, attacking pagans, Jews and heretics, and at Rome held with heretics many private and public disputations.

——— Bede: The Venerable Bede, 672 or 673-735, historian and Doctor of the Church. His greatest work is the *Ecclesiastical History of the English People (Historia Ecclesiastica Gentis Anglorum),* which gives an account of Christianity in England from the beginning until his own era. He deals with science as then understood in *De Natura Rerum, De Temporibus,* and *De Temporum Ratione.*

P. 30. Ultramontanes . . . Council of Trent: Campanella does not employ the term *Ultramontane* with the predominant if not exclusive present-day meaning of pro-Papal. He describes by it members of the Council of Trent who came from "beyond the mountains"; that is, from Spain, France, and other countries located beyond the Alps from Italy. In complete contrast with former and later groups known by the same name, particularly those of nineteenth century France, these Ultramontanes were on the whole anti-Papal. Paolo Sarpi repeatedly uses *Ultramontane* with the meaning employed by Campanella in the well-known work published three years after the *Defense* was composed, the *History of the Council of Trent* (tr. Sir Nathanael Brent [1st ed., 1620], London, 1676, pp. 435, 444, 469, 482, 542, 561, 562, 615, 616 *et cetera*). In the reference first cited, which is given from the Papal point of view Sarpi says in part, "it being discovered that the *Ultramontans* had bad ends and designs, to abate the absolute power which God hath given to the Pope of *Rome,* the more time they have to think on it, the more their Plots will increase." In the passage last cited, the Pope is said to have declared "the practices of the *Italians* in *Trent* were not with his knowledge, but did arise because the *Ultramontans* would tread the Pope[']s authority under their feet." A further passage (p. 634) includes the expression, "not only among the *Spaniards,* but all the *Ultramontanes* also, complaining."

——— Cardinal Bellarmine: Roberto Francesco Bellarmino, 1542-1621, Venerable, distinguished Jesuit theologian, writer, and Cardinal, who c. 1605 became a member of the Holy Office and other congregations, and was perhaps the most important adviser of the Papacy in questions involving theology. As set forth in the *Catholic Encyclopedia,* the Roman Catholic account of the activity of Bellarmine in connection with proscription of heliocentric astronomy by the Sacred Congregation in 1616 says in part that Bellarmine "had always shown great interest in the discoveries of that investigator [Galileo], and was on terms of friendly correspondence with him. He took . . . too—as is witnessed by his letter to Galileo's friend Foscarini—exactly the right attitude towards scientific theories in seeming contradiction with Scripture. If, as was undoubtedly the case then with Galileo's heliocentric theory a scientific theory is insufficiently proved, it should be advanced only as an hypothesis; but if, as is the case with this theory now, care must be taken to interpret Scripture only in accordance with it. When the Holy Office condemned the heliocentric theory, by an excess in the opposite direction, it became Bellarmine's official duty to signify the condemnation to Galileo, and receive his submission."

The statement, "it became Bellarmine's duty to signify the condemnation to Galileo, and receive his submission," is some indication that, as I suggest in the Introduction, n. 6, an important objective of the proscriptive action of the Sacred Congregation was to handicap seriously, if not to suppress, the work of Galileo.

P. 31. Horace: Campanella quotes the *Epistles (Epistulae),* II, i, 83-5, with slight variations from the modern text. He employs *aut* rather than *vel* at the opening of ll. 83-4, and *imberbes* rather than *imberbi* at the opening of l. 85. A comma is used between *sibi* and *ducunt* in l. 83. His version is as follows:

> Aut quia nil rectum, nisi quod placuit sibi, ducunt;
> Aut quia turpe putant, parere minoribus, & quae.
> Imberbes didicere, senes perdenda fateri.

P. 32. Eusebius: Eusebius Pamphili or Eusebius of Caesarea, *c.* 260-*c.* 340, Bishop of Caesarea in Palestine, and the "Father of Church History." His most important work, a masterpiece of erudition, is *Evangelicae Praeparationis Libri XV,* generally known as *Praeparatio Evangelica.* Books IV-VI discuss the chief oracles, worship, and the various beliefs of Greek philosophers on the doctrines of Free Will and Fate; in X-XII it is argued that the Greeks were indebted to the older philosophy and theology of the Hebrews, a point made by Campanella, with emphasis upon the supposed borrowings of Plato from Moses. Campanella may have in mind the extended section which Eusebius devotes to the "vain conceits" of the Greek philosophers (*Praeparatio Evangelica,* tr. E. H. Gifford, Oxford, 1903, III, 899 ff.).

——— Origen: Theologian, teacher, apologist and exegete, 185-253 or 254, to whom Eusebius devotes a major portion of the sixth book of his *Ecclesiastical History.* His *Against Celsus (Contra Celsum)* which Campanella refers to on p. 33 was composed by Origen when he was more than sixty years of age. Celsus was an eclectic Platonist and polemical writer against Christianity who flourished towards the end of the second century. He lived during the reign of Marcus Aurelius, and seemingly did most of his writing between 175 and 180. The work refuted by Origen is *The True Word* or *The True Discourse* against the Christian religion.

P. 33. Alexander: Probably Alexander of Hales, *c.* 1185-1245, Franciscan, theologian, and philosopher, one of the greatest of the scholastics, whose unfinished *Summa Universae Theologiae* was the first "Summary" to make use of Aristotle's physical, metaphysical, and ethical, as well as logical treatises. The commentaries on Aristotle's *Metaphysics* and *De Anima* which were attributed to him during and after Campanella's age, are now assigned to Alexander of Bonini.

——— Saint Vincent: Perhaps Vincent Ferrer, 1350-1419, Saint, Order of Preachers, famous missionary and religious orator. His writings include *De Natura Universalis* and *De Vita Spirituali*. His *Sermons* were published at Antwerp in 1570 and his complete works at Valence in 1591.

—— Master of the *Sentences*: Peter Lombard, *c.* 1100-*c.* 1162, theologian and writer of the famous *Sentences, Quatuor Libri Sententiarum* (*c.* 1150), subsequent to which he was known as "Magister Sententiarum" or simply as "Magister." Campanella employs both titles. His remark that the Holy Spirit does not say what shape Heaven is, was important in stimulating among commentaries upon his work discussion of the extent of the universe and the possibility of a plurality of worlds.

—— Philoponus: John Philoponus, Alexandrian philosopher of the sixth century, a member of the "Tritheists" founded by John Asconagus at the beginning of the century. The followers in time were known as Athanasians or Philoponiaci. Philoponus is the most important sixth century commentator on Aristotle.

P. 35. Simplicius: An Athenian of the fifth century who is perhaps best known for his commentary on Aristotle. Together with Proclus, and with Damascius, whom he accompanied on his exile to Persia *c.* 530, Simplicius was a neo-Platonist.

—— Diodorus of Tarsus: Head of a monastary in or near Antioch and teacher of Saint John Chrysostom, who died about 392. The date of his birth is unknown. Among other works he composed commentaries on the Old Testament, only fragments of which are extant. Diodorus rejected the allegorical interpretation of Scripture employed by the Alexandrines, and defended strongly the literal. As Campanella observes, his disciple Saint John Chrysostom also supported the literal interpretation.

P. 36. Gregory: Perhaps Gregory of Nyssa, died after 385-6, Saint, whose *Treatise on the Work of the Six Days* follows St. Basil's *Hexaemeron*. He treats the Work of the Sixth Day in greater detail in *On the Creation of Man*. St. Gregory was not averse to what has been termed "fine-spun allegorizing."

—— Theophylact: Theophylactus, eleventh century, exegete and Archbishop of Bulgaria, at times known as Theophylactus of Achrida. He was one of the most famous of medieval Greek catenists.

—— That the starry heaven is immobile: An authoritative account of the various cosmological beliefs of the more important Fathers will be found in Giovanni Battista Riccioli, *Almagestum Novum*, Book IX, Section I, "De Substantia . . . Caelorum ac Caelestium Corporum"; Section II, "De Motoribus et Motibus Caelorum"; and Section III, Chapter I, "De Numero Caelorum Totalium" (ed. cit., pp. 193-276, *passim*).

P. 37. Copernicus: The text reads, "Copernicus autem hoc probat ex nomine, quia omnia caelat." The antecedent of "hoc" is "coelum non esse mobile nec rotundum," but for the reason that Copernicus describes heaven as spherical, "hoc" doubtless was intended to refer only to "coelum non esse mobile."

—— Strabo: Greek geographer, born *c.* 63 B. C. at Amasia in Pontus. His *Geography*, probably completed at Rome from materials drawn in large measure from Alexandria, remained for many centuries the leading work in the field.

—— Sixtus Senensis: One of the most noted theologians of the University of Siena, in Tuscany.

P. 42. Athanasius: "Father of Orthodoxy," Bishop of Alexandria, Saint, Confessor and Doctor of the Church, 296-373, one of the great champions of Catholic belief on the subject of the Incarnation. His *Contra Gentes* and *De Incarnatione* were written about 318.

P. 47. Plotinus and Porphyrius: Plotinus, 205-270, a native of Lycopolis in Egypt, the first systematic philosophic exponent of neo-Platonism, a system of idealistic, spiritualistic thought with a tendency toward mysticism which flourished during the early centuries of the Christian era. In 244 Plotinus was teaching philosophy in Rome, and about 263 retired with Porphyrius or Porphyry and other disciples to Campania. His work, consisting of fifty-four treatises, was edited by Porphyry in six groups of nine, and because of this called the "Enneads." The *Enneads* were first published in a Latin translation by Marsilio Ficino, Florence, 1492. Porphyry is generally regarded as surpassing all others of his group in beauty and clearness of style, and in the vigor of his opposition to Christianity. Of his treatises *Against the Christians* only a few fragments are extant. Perhaps the best known of his works is the *Introduction to the Categories of Aristotle,* widely used during the Middle Ages in a Latin translation by Boethius.

P. 48. Empedocles: Famous scientist, philosopher, and doctor born at Agrigentum (Girgenti) in Sicily *c.* 490 B. C., who was influenced deeply by Pythagoreanism and the Orphic Mysteries. He revolted, as Xenophanes, from orthodox theology, and thought of Divinity as existing in living, thinking, and moving substance. His animistic philosophy and his mysticism are not far removed from portions of the thought of Telesio and Campanella. Empedocles died *c.* 435 B. C. in Southern Italy or Greece.

P. 49. Hilary: Probably Hilary of Poitiers, d. 368, Saint, Bishop, whose numerous works were published in Paris, 1693, under the title, *Sancti Hilarii, Pictavorum Episcopi Opera.* . . .

P. 50. Clement of Alexandria: Titus Flavius Clemens, died *c.* 215, early Greek theologian, head of the catechetical school of Alexandria, whose works include the *Outlines, Tutor, Miscellanies,* and *Hortatory Discourse to the Greeks.*

———— Canons of the Church: It is true that the Church had never condemned officially the doctrine of a plurality of worlds. However, as I point out in "The Astronomy of *Paradise Lost,*" *loc. cit.,* p. 239, the doctrine was severely castigated by Eusebius, Hippolytus, and Theoderet, denied by Saint Augustine in the *City of God,* and placed by him in his book of heresies *(De Haeresibus ad Quodvuldeum Liber Unus).* Saint Isidore of Seville did likewise in the seventh century, and the canon containing his condemnation was repeated in the codification of Anselmus Lucensis, and in the *Concordia Discordantium Canonum* (*c.* 1144) compiled by Gratian and generally known as the *Decretum.*

P. 51. Democritus and Epicurus: There is at present some difference of opinion as to whether the infinite worlds of Democritus and other Grecian philosophers were regarded by them as co-existent or as sequential. At the time of Campanella, the infinite worlds generally were regarded as co-existent.

———— The articles . . . University of Paris: See note on "Articles" of p. 24, above. Campanella refers here to number thirty-four of the condemned propositions, that God could not create a plurality of worlds ("Quod Prima Causa non posset plures mundos facere.").

P. 52. Insanity of Paracelsus. See text, p. 8. Theophrastus Paracelsus, 1493-1541, celebrated physician and reformer of therapeutics, also known as Theophrastus Bombastus von Hohenheim. He once burned the works of Avicenna in the public square. His own writings are characterized by a simple, direct, and understandable style.

P. 54. I find no authority for Campanella's statement that Pope Paul III gave permission for the printing of the *Revolutions* of Copernicus.

P. 55. Pope Gelasius: Gelasius I, d. 496, Saint, who published at a Roman synod in 494 his famous *Catalogue* of the authentic writings of the Fathers, and a list of apocryphal and interpolated works. A further section of the *Catalogue* was devoted to the proscribed books of heretics. I have interpreted Campanella's citation, "dist. 15. c. *Sancta Romana,*" to refer to that part of the *Catalogue* devoted to the writings of the Fathers.

P. 56. Laertius: Diogenes Laertius, author of the famous *Lives of the Philosophers.*

———— Timaeus Locrus: Campanella appears mistaken when he ascribes to this unknown neo-Platonist (not the Timaeus of Lokri whom Plato introduces as the leading character in the dialogue named after him) as an advocate of the diurnal rotation of the earth (*cf. Timaeus Locrus,* 79D). Philolaus believed both earth and Sun turned about a central fire.

———— Pherecydes of Syra: Pherecydes of the Island of Cyra of the Cyclades in the Ægean Sea, fl. 544 B. C., philosopher and teacher of Pythagoras. In his cosmogony, "Zeus and Chronos and Chthonia . . . are the three first beginnings. . . . Then Chronos produced out of himself fire, air, and water." Chthonia appears to be the moist Proto-matter —neither sea nor good dry land, in Milton's words—out of which Ge, or the earth, is created.

P. 57. Denys the Carthusian, termed by Campanella "Dionysius Carthusianus": Denys van Leeuwen, 1402-1471, the last important encyclopedic writer among the scholastics, whose favorite author was Dionysius the Areopagite. As a mystical writer he resembles Hugh and Richard of St. Victor, and St. Bonaventure. At the request of Nicolas Cardinal of Cusa he wrote two treatises against Mohammedanism, *Contra Perfidiam Mahometi,* to which Campanella refers.

INDEX

Abdia of Judea, 73
Adam, 18, 36
Adami, Tobia, vii
Albenragel, 28
Albergotti, Ulisse, 35, 84
Albertus Magnus, ix, xii, 15, 36, 79-80
Albumasar, 28, 83
Alexander (of Hales?), 41, 86
Alexander Aphrodisaeus, 45
Alfarabius, 28, 83
Alfonso, King, 23, 73, 82
Ambrose, Saint, 12, 23, 33, 36, 40-3, 52-4, 58, 61, 64, 72-3, 78
Anastasius of Sinai, 16, 27, 74, 80
Anaxagoras, 19, 29, 62
Ancients and Moderns controversy, xxix, xxxviii ff.
Anthony, Saint, 24, 42, 81
Antipodes, xxvi, 15, 35, 51, 79
Apelles, Fictus, 11
Argus, 10
Aristarchus, xxxviii, 51
Aristotle (Aristotelian, Aristotelians), xii, xvii, xxviii, xxxii, xxxix, xlii-iii, 6 ff., passim
Ashmole, Elias, xli
Astrology, 32
Athanasius, Saint, 53, 87
Augustine, Saint, xxvi, xxxvi, 15, 18, 27, 31, 33-7, 40-6, 48, 50-2, 55-6, 58-64, 67, 74, 80
Averroes (Averroists), 28, 30, 41-2, 60, 83
Avicenna, 15, 28, 36, 80
Axiochus, v. Ficino, Marsilio

Bacon, Sir Francis, xi and n., xxx-i, xlii and n.
Baranzano, Redento, 4, 77
Barlow, William, xxiii
Barnabus, Apostle, 26, 83
Baron, Vincent, xii
Barrius Franciscanus, 72
Barthelemy the Englishman, xxxviii
Basil, Saint, 23, 40, 42-3, 46, 49, 56-9, 61-4, 82
Bede, the Venerable, 36, 46, 48, 52, 58, 61, 74, 85
Bellarmine, Cardinal, vii and viii n., 37, 74, 85-6
Bembo, 31, 84
Bernard, Saint, 14, 19, 24-6, 39, 42-3, 79
Berosus, 20, 82

Bonaventure, Saint, 58
Book of God (Nature), 21, 24-5, 28, 30, 42, 52
Boterus, 28
Boyle, Robert, xxxiv and n.
Brahe, Tycho, xvii-xix and n., xxv, xxxi, xxxviii, 63, 70
Brigid, Saint, 19, 81
Bruno, Giordano, viii n., 4, 11, 67
Burton, Robert, xli

Caesar, Julius, la Galla, xxiv
Cajetan, Cardinal, 33, 66, 84
Calippus, 23, 82
Calvin, John, xxi
Campanella, Tommaso, life and thought, ix ff., xxxi ff., xxxv ff., xxxix ff., 4
Capella, Martianus, xxxviii
Cardan (Carden), Girolamo, xxxi
Caselli, Tommaso, 12, 78
Castelli, Benedetto, vii
Cato, 9, 29, 68, 77
Celsus, 41
Christ, 16, 20, 25-6, 29, 31, 52, 64, 67, 74
Chrysostom, Saint, 18, 19, 24-5, 27, 29, 33, 36, 40, 42-6, 48-9, 51-2, 54-5, 57, 59, 61, 81
Cicero, 14
Clavius, Christopher, xxii, 11, 78
Clement of Alexandria, 64, 88
Clement, Saint, of Rome, 25, 64, 83
Columbus, 35, 42
Comenius (Komenski), Bishop John Amos, ix, xli ff.
Comets, xvii, 12
Congregation, Sacred, viii and n., xx
Copernican astronomy, xxii, xxvi-viii, xxxvii, 4 ff., passim; its heresy, xiv ff.
Copernicus, Nicolaus, xii, xv ff., xxvi, xxx-i, xxxviii, 4, 10, and passim
Cotherinus, 64
Crane, Ronald S., xxxvi-vii
Cusanus (Cusa), Nicolas, Cardinal, viii n., xxxix and n., 4, 11, 51, 67
Cyprian, Saint, 71
Cyril, Saint, 19, 25, 42, 81

Dante, 35
David, 19, 20, 35, 44, 46, 50, 56, 62, 64, 68-9, 74
Defense of Galileo, date of composition, vii and n., viii n.

[91]

Delrio, Martin, 8, 77
Democritus, 65, 88
Denys the Carthusian, 73-4, 89
Descartes, René, xi, xii *n*.
Didacus à Stunica (Stuniga), viii *n*.,
    xxiv, xxv *n*.
Digges, Thomas, xvi-viii
Diodorus, Bishop of Tarsus, 44-6
Dionysius, Bishop, 18, 80
Domenico Maria da Novara, 11, 12,
    51, 73, 78

Earth, situation, motion etc., 5, 7 ff.,
    44 ff., 52, 64, 70
Ecphantus, xxxviii
Empedocles, xii, 56, 62-4, 74, 88
Empirical epistemology, xxix ff.
Empyrean, xiv ff., 57, 59, 60
Ephrem, Saint, 15, 35, 42, 80
Epicurus, 41, 54, 65, 88
Eudoxus, 23, 82
Eugene III, 24, 82
Eusebius, 40, 44-6, 72, 86

Failla, Jacopo, vii *n*.
Fantoni, Sebastiano, 4
Fathers (Church), 17, 18, 24, 27,
    31, 35-6, 42-6, 48-9, 52, 58, 68, 69
Ficino, Marsilio, 57, 81-2
Firmament, 12, 13, 46 ff., 56 ff.
Foscarini, Paolo Antonio, ix *n*., xxv-
    viii, 4
Francesco Maria of Ferrara, *v.*
    Domenico Maria
Fuller, Nicholas, xxiii

Gaetani, Boniface Cardinal, 5, 75, 77
Galen, 72
Gelasius I, 71, 88
Galilei, Galileo, vii, viii *n*., xi, xii,
    xviii, xix, xxv, xxvii-viii, xxx ff.,
    4 ff., *passim*
Gilbert, William, viii *n*., xviii, xxv,
    xxxi, 4, 11, 51
Goodman, Godfrey, xxxix
Gregory I (The Great), Saint, 18,
    21, 33, 46, 61, 67, 81

Haly, 28, 83
Heaven, *v.* Sphere, Eighth
Hell, location etc., 44-5, 50
Heraclides of Pontus, xxxviii, 51
Hilary, Saint, 64, 88
Hill, Nicolas, 4, 77
Hill, Thomas, xxii-iii
Höffding, Harald, xxxiii
Holy Office, *v.* Inquisition
Horace, 38, 86

Inquisition, vii, viii *n*.
Isidore, Saint, 35, 85

Jerome, Saint, 18, 31, 39, 61, 64, 80
Job, 21, 24, 32, 51, 74
Jones, Richard F., xxxix, xlii *n*.
Joseph, 74
Josephus, 20, 27, 64, 82
Julian, the Apostate, 19, 32, 81
Justin, Saint, 13, 15, 40-1, 43-6, 79

Kepler, John, viii *n*., xxv-vi, xxx-i,
    4, 11, 51, 67

Lactantius, Lucius, xxvi, 15, 20, 35,
    42, 44-5, 48, 51, 81
Laertius, Diogenes, 72, 89
Lateran Council, 17, 28-9, 31, 80
Leo I, 14, 19, 24, 25, 30, 79
Leo X, 17, 28, 80
Leonardo da Vinci, xxx
Livy, 14-15
Locke, John, xxx, xxxiii-iv
Lombard, Peter, 42, 44, 47-9, 55,
    58-9, 68, 87
Lucretius, 54
Luke, Apostle, 20, 67
Luther, Martin, xxi, 67
Lyncean philosophers, 3, 77

Machiavelli (Machiavellians, Machia-
    vellianism), 20-1, 32, 42, 84
Maestlin, Michael, viii *n*, xvii, 4,
    10, 51
Magellan, 42
Magini, Giovanni Antonio, 11, 51
Magister; Master of the Sentences,
    v. Lombard, Peter
Medicean planets, 52, 70
Melanchthon, Philip, xxi
Mersenne, Marin, xli
Merton, Robert K., xxxiii *n*.
Milton, John, xvi *n*.
Mirandola, Antonio, 30, 84
Mirandola, Giovanni Pico della, 12,
    72, 78
Mohammed (Mohammedans), 8, 36,
    65, 73-4
Moon, composition etc., 8, 28, 52,
    54, 61, 64-5, 73
More, Henry, xxxvii *n*.
Moses, 12, 16, 18, 25-6, 28, 39, 46,
    48, 52, 57, 59, 60, 62-3, 72-3, 83
Moses, Bishop of Syria, 16, 80

Nature, *v.* Book of God
Newton, Sir Isaac, xxxiv, xxxvii
Nicaea, Council of, 29
Nicephorus, 19, 42
Nicetas, xxxviii
Nicolson, Marjorie, viii *n*.
Nolanus, *v.* Bruno, Giordano
Novara, *v.* Domenico Maria
Numa Pompilius, 12

Origanus (Tost), David, xxxviii, 4
Origen, 33, 40-1, 43, 45, 52, 56, 61-2, 86
Overbury, Thomas, xxiii *n.*
Ovid, 12, 20, 45, 68, 81

Pallavicini, Cardinal, xii
Pammachius, 31, 84
Paracelsus, xxx-i, 8, 67, 88
Paradise, Earthly, 38, 44
Paris, Articles condemned at (1277), 29, 40, 66, 71, 83, 88
Patrizio (Patrizzi), Francesco, 4
Paul, Apostle, 14, 17, 18, 21, 24, 30, 44, 46
Paul III, xxi, 10, 71, 78
Peter, Apostle, 21, 25, 44, 64
Pherecydes of Syra, 73, 89
Philastrius, Saint, 36, 51, 85
Philo the Jew, 20, 27, 64, 82
Philolaus, 51, 89
Philoponus, 43, 87
Philosophy, 16, 26, 28, 31, 34, 42, 73
Pineda, John, xxiv
Plato, xii, xl and n., 14, 20, 25-6, 29, 40, 45, 57, 59, 61
Pliny, 12, 14, 55
Plotinus, 60-1, 87
Plutarch, 72
Porphyrius, 60, 63, 72, 87
Pomponazzi, Pietro, x, 80
Procopius Gaza, 35, 44-6, 48, 52, 61, 84
Progress, Idea of, xxix, xxxv ff.
Ptolemy (Ptolemists etc.), xiv ff., 11 ff., 23, 30, 51 and *passim*
Purchas, Samuel, xxiii *n.*
Pythagoras (Pythagorean, Pythagoreans), xii, xxxix and n., 4, 11, 12, 23, 45, 51, 55, 56, 61-2, 64, 70-4

Rabbis, 27, 41, 62, 73-4
Ramus, Peter (Pierre de la Ramée), xxxi
Reformation and Counter-Reformation, xiii-iv
Reinhold, Erasmus, 10, 11, 51
Reymers, Nicolas, xviii, xxv *n.*, xxxi, xxxviii
Rheticus, Georg Joachim, xx and n., xxx, 4
Riccioli, Giovanni Battista, viii *n.*
Richard of Saint Victor, 24, 82
Ridley, Marke, xxiii, xxxviii
Roeslin, Helisaeus, xxiv
Rothmann, Christopher, xxv, 10

Scholastics, 43-4, 68
Schonberg, Nicolas Cardinal, 10, 78

Scientific Movement, modern, xiii and n.
Scoriggio, Lazzaro, 4, 77
Scriptural literalism and heliocentric astronomy, conflict between, xx ff., 5 ff., *passim*
Serafinus de Firmo, 41
Shakleton, Francis, xxxix
Simplicius, 22, 43, 48, 87
Sixtus Senensis, 47-8, 64, 73, 87
Socrates, 29
Solomon, 19, 21, 24, 30, 50-2, 63, 72, 74
Sphere, Eighth (Heaven), xiv, xvi ff., 7, 11, 12, 42 ff., 55, 60, 64, 70, 74
Stadius, John, 10, 51, 78
Stars, New, 12, 63, 70
Starry Messenger (Sidereus Nuncius), 4, 11, 67
Stars, composition etc., 8, 11, 12, 48-9, 52, 54-5, 58, 62, 64, 70, 73
Stelliola, Colantonus, 51
Stoics, 40
Strabo, 46, 48, 87
Stunica, *v.* Didacus à Stunica
Sun, composition and place, 7 ff., 43, 51-6, 70

Telescope, 3, 37
Telesio, Bernardino, ix, x, xii, xxxi, 55, 59, 70
Terence, 16, 80
Thebit, 23, 73, 82
Theodoret, 42
Theophylact, 45, 87
Timaeus Locrus, 73
Thomas Aquinas, Saint, ix, xii, xxxvi, 7, 15-18, 22-3, 27-9, 31-4, 36-7, 39-52, 55-62, 65-8, 71, 73, 74, 79
Trent, Council of, 37, 85
Tyrell, James, xxxiii

Vincent Ferrer, Saint, 41, 86
Vitruvius, xxxviii
Vives, Ludovicus, xli *n.*, xlii
Volz, John R., xi

Wilkins, Bishop John, ix, xxxii-iv, xxxvii *n.*, xliii-iv, 83
Worlds, Plurality of, 8, 11, 12, 56, 61, 63-6, 73
Wright, Edward, xxv

Xenophanes, 35, 37, 51, 85
Xenophon, 14, 20

Zeno, xii
Zenocrates, 60

HISTORY, PHILOSOPHY AND SOCIOLOGY OF SCIENCE

Classics, Staples and Precursors

An Arno Press Collection

Aliotta, [Antonio]. **The Idealistic Reaction Against Science.** 1914

Arago, [Dominique François Jean]. **Historical Eloge of James Watt.** 1839

Bavink, Bernhard. **The Natural Sciences.** 1932

Benjamin, Park. **A History of Electricity.** 1898

Bennett, Jesse Lee. **The Diffusion of Science.** 1942

[Bronfenbrenner], Ornstein, Martha. **The Role of Scientific Societies in the Seventeenth Century.** 1928

Bush, Vannevar. **Endless Horizons.** 1946

Campanella, Thomas. **The Defense of Galileo.** 1937

Carmichael, R. D. **The Logic of Discovery.** 1930

Caullery, Maurice. **French Science and its Principal Discoveries Since the Seventeenth Century.** [1934]

Caullery, Maurice. **Universities and Scientific Life in the United States.** 1922

Debates on the Decline of Science. 1975

de Beer, G. R. **Sir Hans Sloane and the British Museum.** 1953

Dissertations on the Progress of Knowledge. [1824]. 2 vols. in one

Euler, [Leonard]. **Letters of Euler.** 1833. 2 vols. in one

Flint, Robert. **Philosophy as Scientia Scientiarum and a History of Classifications of the Sciences.** 1904

Forke, Alfred. **The World-Conception of the Chinese.** 1925

Frank, Philipp. **Modern Science and its Philosophy.** 1949

The Freedom of Science. 1975

George, William H. **The Scientist in Action.** 1936

Goodfield, G. J. **The Growth of Scientific Physiology.** 1960

Graves, Robert Perceval. **Life of Sir William Rowan Hamilton.** 3 vols. 1882

Haldane, J. B. S. Science and Everyday Life. 1940

Hall, Daniel, et al. The Frustration of Science. 1935

Halley, Edmond. Correspondence and Papers of Edmond Halley. 1932

Jones, Bence. The Royal Institution. 1871

Kaplan, Norman. Science and Society. 1965

Levy, H. The Universe of Science. 1933

Marchant, James. Alfred Russel Wallace. 1916

McKie, Douglas and Niels H. de V. Heathcote. The Discovery of Specific and Latent Heats. 1935

Montagu, M. F. Ashley. Studies and Essays in the History of Science and Learning. [1944]

Morgan, John. A Discourse Upon the Institution of Medical Schools in America. 1765

Mottelay, Paul Fleury. Bibliographical History of Electricity and Magnetism Chronologically Arranged. 1922

Muir, M. M. Pattison. A History of Chemical Theories and Laws. 1907

National Council of American-Soviet Friendship. Science in Soviet Russia: Papers Presented at Congress of American-Soviet Friendship. 1944

Needham, Joseph. A History of Embryology. 1959

Needham, Joseph and Walter Pagel. Background to Modern Science. 1940

Osborn, Henry Fairfield. From the Greeks to Darwin. 1929

Partington, J[ames] R[iddick]. Origins and Development of Applied Chemistry. 1935

Polanyi, M[ichael]. The Contempt of Freedom. 1940

Priestley, Joseph. Disquisitions Relating to Matter and Spirit. 1777

Ray, John. The Correspondence of John Ray. 1848

Richet, Charles. The Natural History of a Savant. 1927

Schuster, Arthur. The Progress of Physics During 33 Years (1875-1908). 1911

Science, Internationalism and War. 1975

Selye, Hans. From Dream to Discovery: On Being a Scientist. 1964

Singer, Charles. Studies in the History and Method of Science. 1917/1921. 2 vols. in one

Smith, Edward. **The Life of Sir Joseph Banks.** 1911

Snow, A. J. **Matter and Gravity in Newton's Physical Philosophy.** 1926

Somerville, Mary. **On the Connexion of the Physical Sciences.** 1846

Thomson, J. J. **Recollections and Reflections.** 1936

Thomson, Thomas. **The History of Chemistry.** 1830/31

Underwood, E. Ashworth. **Science, Medicine and History.** 2 vols. 1953

Visher, Stephen Sargent. **Scientists Starred 1903-1943 in American Men of Science.** 1947

Von Humboldt, Alexander. **Views of Nature: Or Contemplations on the Sublime Phenomena of Creation.** 1850

Von Meyer, Ernst. **A History of Chemistry from Earliest Times to the Present Day.** 1891

Walker, Helen M. **Studies in the History of Statistical Method.** 1929

Watson, David Lindsay. **Scientists Are Human.** 1938

Weld, Charles Richard. **A History of the Royal Society.** 1848. 2 vols. in one

Wilson, George. **The Life of the Honorable Henry Cavendish.** 1851

DATE DUE